'Little Bobby'

STICKS AND COAL

By

Geoff Whalley

Published by

MELROSE BOOKS

An Imprint of Melrose Press Limited
St Thomas Place, Ely
Cambridgeshire
CB7 4GG, UK
www.melrosebooks.co.uk

FIRST EDITION

Cover designed by Melrose Books

ISBN   978-1-909757-46-2

Printed and bound in Great Britain by:
Bell & Bain Limited, Glasgow

This book is dedicated to the memory of Marjorie Whalley and her son Robert Conway Whalley ("Little Bobby")

My mum, Marjorie Whalley, to whom this book is dedicated

CONTENTS

FOREWORD

'You know LARK RISE TO CANDLEFORD? Well, that's just a story created for television. My family really lived that sort of country village life—not fiction, but fact!'

Those were more or less the words that Geoff Whalley used to describe to me the book he was in the process of writing about the fascinating life of his family members over the past century. Their story was his, in that he was born in the same beautiful corner of north west England that had been the family's home for generations—Croston, near Preston in Lancashire, which even today, has been surprisingly untouched by the march of time.

Some people telling the story not just of a family, but a community, would tell it from the point of view of the local minister or shop keeper—but Geoff's family had just as unique, although definitely more unusual, opportunity to share the comings and goings of local life. They were the village undertakers, a role in which Geoff still takes great pride today. This is more than just a business for him. He loves this community. He knows its families. His friends are here, in the lanes, the shops and the churches—and church life has always marked the joys and sorrows of the congregations it serves. This is a village with a centuries-old church which has probably not changed in essence from the day it first opened its doors. Faith underpins everything here, perhaps because a community which works on and lives alongside the beauty of God's creation, with all its raw, challenging beauty, is constantly aware of the presence and power of God both in the world around them, and in the depths of their own hearts.

Geoff has a deep love and loyalty to the past, but he worries about the future. In particular, he is concerned that future generations have the chance to learn the truth of the Christian Gospel which has been the mainstay of his own existence. For that reason, he has not only established a peaceful meadow and woodland burial ground in Much Hoole consecrated for those of all faiths, but he has built and had dedicated God's Acre Chapel, which also has an education centre for all to study the Bible and discuss its essential relevance for us today.

Geoff is a passionate man—passionate about his roots, his ancestors, his family, his community and his faith. He is a shining example of true Christianity, humble, hardworking and constant. I have felt privileged to get to know him and his family over the years.

I commend this evocative and warm-hearted book to everyone— because it's a good book written by a very good man.

Pam Rhodes

PREFACE

I suppose, for the purposes of this book, that my humble life begins in Cheshire around the Tatton Park district in the 1880s, where both the males, George Whalley and Joe Royle, worked, George being a farm labourer, and Joe being a shire horse stallion man. At that time the owner was Lord Edgerton, who was to become the leading person in forming the Shire Cart Horse Society (and five years later the newly named Shire Horse Society). He won the National Championship, and no doubt Joe was involved. Little did Joe realise that, some 100 years on, his grandson would have the fourth biggest stud in all of Lancashire.

My Grandad, Joe Royle, met Grandma Frances when they both worked for Lord Edgerton on the Tatton Hall Estate in Cheshire. Indeed, Grandad Whalley also worked there. Neither recollected knowing each other. Those of you who have watched the television drama *Mr Selfridge* will have noticed the name Lord Edgerton taking a prominent role regarding the First World War. In 2012, I visited the farm, and Hall—which is still as it would have been then—and I walked up the stairs to the farm office just as it would have been when my grandparents received their wages. Just down the road in High Legh, at Mill House Farm, lived the future icon of the family, Sylvia Stringer (she being the daughter of David Stringer), and her siblings. One of my relatives, Beryl Hume, now has a travel business in Knutsford, and I only found and spoke to her last autumn. What a small world.

BACKGROUND TO MY MOTHER'S FAMILY

It would seem that Grandad and Grandma Royle had eleven children, but unfortunately they did seem to have (not unlike a coal mine) a seam of unhappiness running through their family, so I would like to share it with you if I may.

Of the eleven children, Reg, the eldest, lost a son to cancer in his late twenties. Uncle Wilfred, aged seventeen years, became an apprentice butcher, loved his sport and, whilst playing for Burscough, got struck on his knee with one of those heavy leather balls, and over a matter of three to four weeks developed Bright's Disease and died. It came as a great shock to his mum and dad. Uncle Percy wasn't having any of this farming lark, and at one time became chauffeur to Mrs Thompson at Blackpool Fairground; and, indeed, the Royle family became good friends of the Thompsons. I think they used to graze their donkeys at Grandad's. Uncle Harry went to work at an electrical firm in London. One day a workmate discarded his cigarette stub and it landed in some petrol, ignited, and severely burnt him. He had to be nursed a long time at home by his mum. He, too, became a chauffeur for his dad's employer, Mr Thorougood. It was a true story that he was allowed to take the posh car on his honeymoon only if he would take Mr Thorougood's prize racing pigeons fastened to the back of the car and release them at Frodsham, which was an important releasing place for racing pigeons and still is. He was called up to go to war, but sadly taken prisoner at Tobruk, and was in prison for nearly the full length of the war in Germany where he suffered greatly, until released by the Russians. Uncle Harry's wife, Marion, had both legs removed later in life. His son, Gerald, was killed at only forty-nine years of age when his lorry jackknifed.

Uncle Jack was a good worker, and my Mum used to say she could work with him best. He had three children: John was the eldest, then Barbara, and Phillip. I spent a lot of time with Uncle Jack and Aunty Kitty after my Dad died, working on the farm. I lived on Weetabix, and with them always having plenty of milk, it was a good place to be. I was just old enough to drive a tractor, which pleased me. Barbara was born with a deformity of the spine and no thumb or elbow on her right arm. She had to go to Manchester Children's Hospital and Oswestry Orthopaedic Hospital for many lengthy stays and operations, and needed a surgical corset to help her stay straight. How she suffered with it rubbing her raw! She would come into the building and watch me work, and talk as if she was a mature lady; as brave a lass as you would ever meet. Her brother Phillip was always quiet, and death was to surface twice in that household: Barbara at twenty-one, and Phillip aged about fifty-six. I still see John at family gatherings—still the same; a nice fellow.

Frances was next to be born, and was a perfect baby. A few weeks later, her mum, also Frances, decided that, for her first outing, she would go to Ormskirk Market. She left Auntie in charge of the baby. Auntie was lame, and unfortunately stumbled while holding the baby, and dropped the child upon the flagged floor. Frances was told of the incident, and for a few days it was thought that no harm had been done. Frances and Joe realized later that something was wrong, saw their GP, and were referred to a specialist at Liverpool. Young Frances was diagnosed as having brain damage, and was to never develop further. She was always strapped in a chair, and started to have fits. She grew up in body but not in mind. She never showed any sign of recognition, lived until she was eleven years of age, and died after a massive fit. Although a great burden to her mum and dad, they were heartbroken when she died. She was loved by everybody and was never forgotten. This terrible seam was still continuing its way through the family.

My Mum, Marjorie, came next, and was involved in much tragedy. And as this book is dedicated to her and her little son, Robert Conway Whalley ('Little Bobby'), I will deal with this later in a chapter of its own.

Then came Aunty Barbara. She was always outgoing, and involved in all kinds of organisations. She met a young man called Bill Banks from Eccleston, near Chorley, who always had a cough problem. They had arranged the wedding date, but he was taken ill a few weeks before so they saw a specialist, and he told her, secretly, that Bill only had a year to live. The specialist asked Aunty Barbara if he should tell Bill, and she said no, but she also asked Bill's dad's advice (his mother having died) and he agreed that it should be kept secret. Barbara and Bill were happily married for two and a half years, and then he died aged twenty-seven.

The twins were next: George and Leonard. Uncle Len didn't have children and both he and his wife Ethel died a little while ago. Uncle George and his wife Edna had a son Malcolm, who I see from time to time. Both George and Edna died some years ago.

When you go through this part of the family in detail, not including deaths through natural aging, it surely had its fair share of trouble, losing three daughters, one son, two sons-in-law, and six grandsons, all fairly young.

George Whalley went on to meet Sylvia Stringer, and they married in due course. What a driving and demanding force she was to become, ruling her family with an iron fist!

My grandmother

One of their first decisions in married life was to move from Cheshire to take on a rundown small farm on a bleak hill overlooking Blackburn; and, surprisingly, ninety years later, every time I look out of my back windows I can see this hillside, which is known as 'Darwen Towers'. It must have been a most inhospitable place to live, and would have had no electricity or running water. My grandparents had to carry water by hand from a spring for all their animals—and, of course, for private use—but having known my grandmother, she would cope as well as bring her children up.

In the 1930s they moved to the village of Croston (near to Chorley, Leyland and Preston), a thriving place which is mentioned in the Domesday Book, a place that was to mean a great deal to me, but which, unfortunately, also brought much sadness. The Royles also moved to Croston at about the same time. This move had a great bearing on what was to come in the future.

The Hillocks, Croston

The River Yarrow, Croston

The infant school where I attended

Church Street, Croston

Church Street, Croston - St Michael's Church

Church Street, Croston - Town Bridge Farm where I was born

Croston was a special place in that it supported seven pubs, a very old church (St Michael and All Angels'), Croston Methodist Chapel, two Primitive Chapels, and two large factories (one, textiles, and one which later made pot urinals and flush toilets). It also had its own gasworks, and up until 1948 it had its own District Council. There were many rows of terraced cottages (some of which are still there today), some being directly behind others or indeed built onto backs of houses. There was quite a large river which divided part of the village and bypassed the church and infants' school, and which seemed to flood twice a year. At the time, when I was a young lad, there was a Bishop of Whalley (no connection with us), who resided in Croston; plus there was a large rectory. The Church of England was also a mother church to surrounding village churches, and to this day the Rawstorne family has the gift of the living of Croston, St Mary's Church, Penwortham, and St Andrew's Church, Longton. Croston also had a large police station, and its own courtroom and cells.

We were indeed fortunate to have a lovely Squire by the name of Humphrey de Trafford, who lived in an old hall with his sister, Miss Hermy, and who found work for many poor families in Croston. He once told us that he was the poor relative of the Manchester 'de Traffords'! There was a private chapel, attached to the hall, which was re-opened for use by the Catholic people of Croston, and which, at the time of writing, is now closed; and the hall has now been knocked down. In Cardinal Hulme's memories (in a TV programme) he tells how this old man came into his office and handed all the deeds over to him. I will always regret their decision to knock it down. Miss Hermy was a well-known breeder of rabbits and could often be seen collecting dandelion leaves from under the hedgerows. Croston people owe a great deal of gratitude to the Squire and his sister for helping poor people, providing them with work and lower rents.

Following the courtship and marriage of Percy Whalley (George's son) and Marjorie, they were able to get the tenancy of a railway cottage right next to the line. Those cottages were intended to be for farm labourers with their wives opening the big crossing gates, for in those days it was mostly horses and lorries passing through.

Great happiness was given to Mum and Dad with the arrival of a beautiful baby boy, Robert Conway Whalley, the middle name being a legacy of the local GP who, of course, was there at the birth. Robert was then, and forever, called 'Little Bobby'. Dad would surely have said, as he was to say many times, that he would be a farmer (as he said to us later as we came onto the scene). Sorry to say that Mum's joy would not last two years before she would lose a child. Also, in the next twelve years, close relatives, a husband, and two of her children would have serious illnesses. Much later, one of her grandchildren would have cancer as well.

That poor woman! God must have had a duty for her somewhere else as, right out of the blue, she had the most awful death (which I will go into later).

Getting back to Mum and Dad, they enjoyed this little boy so much. Then Mum found out she was pregnant again (as was usual in those days). She would have the baby at home in—if you can imagine—this little cottage, the railway passing within twenty-five feet of it. When she looked out of the kitchen window she could see Dad's parents' farm 400 yards away, and if she opened the front door, 600 yards away she could see her parents' farm. There were no hedges about, and life could not have been sweeter, but it was to change!

It was decided that Little Bobby was to go to Mum's mother's while she had the baby (as I said, 600 yards away).

Mum seemed, so I was told, to have difficult births, and this was no exception. Anyway, a baby girl was born, to be named Nancy, so they now had the perfect family. Nancy's name must have come from mother's side, from one of her elder sisters who was never well.

Sadly, within a few days, word reached them that Little Bobby was unwell. I suppose that in those days a lot of children got colds, as they do today, but with no antibiotics it was usually a cough medicine bottle, that always had that lovely taste of spinach, purchased from this new chemist man, Mr Kelly (Henry), who was a good friend of Mum's brother Jack. Sorry to say it didn't cure Bobby, so he was rushed from his grandparents' farm to hospital, where he died on the 3rd November 1942 (aged two) in the Isolation Hospital, having been moved from the old Royal Preston Hospital.

For those who can remember the hospital, it had a big reception area, straight through the main doors, where you sat for hours waiting your turn, whether it was for a clinic appointment or to see the Casualty doctors—one of whom was a fairly large doctor, Dr Cank, who seemed to talk to you and others very loudly; his voice seemed to bellow out everywhere, in many ways similar to Mum's dad, Joe Royle.

Dr Cank would probably be a doctor for the battlefields—cut your leg off as soon as look at you! Remarkably, he came from Croston too, and his family were well known to us all.

Mother was never certain that the diagnosis was correct, but paratyphoid fever (similar to typhoid fever) was put on the death certificate. I am not sure if Mum was with him when he died, as some children were kept in total isolation on wards and you were not encouraged to visit.

My Dad's mother instructed the local undertaker, Mr Coxhead of Coxhead and Bretherton, to carry out Little Bobby's funeral, which was held at St Michael and All Angels' Church, Croston, and burial in the churchyard. There were, in those days, quite a lot of children's deaths, but what made this one unusual was that my parents were told that, because of the infection, the coffin could not go inside the cottage. However, my Grandma Whalley, being the type of person she was, would have none of that, so she asked Mr Coxhead to put a glass window in the lid of the coffin so that all could view him. My mother was to tell me later that she wished that had not been done and, from my experience later in life, little children lose their bloom quickly. No embalming and make-up was available in those days. That railway cottage has never altered, even now having a porch covering the front door, and it may still be a railway property.

With the German fighter aircraft using the railway line as a sort of radar line to find the port of Preston, they regularly flew over my parents' cottage, which, incidentally, was called 'High Lane Crossing'.

Actually, all the farmers called what people today would call 'The Moss' the Finney. I am not sure why. Also, those large bulks of timber called stocks used to work their way to the surface and probably break a part of the plough. They are still there today, stacked up on the headland, sixty-five years later, and only just showing signs of rotting away; they would be hundreds of years old. All in all, it was a very stressful time for both my parents.

Not long after the loss of Little Bobby, the Squire of Croston, Mr Humphrey de Trafford, called to see my grandparents at the farm where Dad worked, and saw my grandmother, Sylvia, still carrying buckets of water for the animals and humans. He told her of the impending vacancy of a farm in the village. The farm was called Town Bridge Farm, and the family of Daltons had been tenants, and had given their notice. He told her she would not need to carry water as it had mains water.

Eventually, Grandad and Grandmother moved into Town Bridge Farm, together with us all. Two years later, one Sunday evening—16th July 1944—as the bells rang out, I was born, with a head of blonde curly hair; a further farmer, as I had replaced Little Bobby.

I really think my arrival helped my parents to get over losing a son so, of course, I took Bobby's middle name and thus was christened Geoffrey Conway Whalley, and in the church records my father wrongly gave my date of birth as 26th July 1944!

All went well for a while; then my grandfather died, and for some reason he was put in the same grave as Little Bobby, thus meaning he would never be with his parents. That, of course, later concerned my mother, a situation that was to rear its head again with far greater repercussions for Mum (again, which I will deal with later).

Within two and a half years (I was their third child) I had an enlarged lump in my neck which turned out to be a TB-infected gland, which had to be sorted out. In those days you had to have sunlight treatment on it. I am not sure what that did, but I suppose it shrivelled the TB up. The difficulty was that for two years, three times a week, my mother had to take me fifteen miles each way, on and off four buses, to Preston

'Little Bobby'

Hospital, which coincided with two terrible winters (one of them in 1947 had snowdrifts four to six feet deep; prisoners of war were used to clear the roads). Mum used to say that I enjoyed the travelling, and when we got home I used to tell them we went up and down and up and down because of the bridges that we went over. I loved rocking chairs, and from a very early age, when Mum was out helping Dad on the farm, Grandmother would give me a piece of toast, tell me to sit on the rocking chair and not to move. Mum began to get worried that I was forever rocking on this chair and they had to stop me as it was becoming a habit. I think they also knew that the children in hospitals used to do this as it gave them comfort when they suffered serious long-term illness.

In the meantime, Edwin Percy Whalley came in 1947, but all the time Nancy continued to suffer with her tonsils and ears. Her ears discharged the most horrible stuff; it would be on the pillows even when cotton wool had been packed in them. This went on throughout her infancy, and eventually she was to have her tonsils out, which seemed to make a great improvement to her health and she never looked back.

I started school nearly next door to where we lived, and found it hard going. I was shy, and later in life I came to the opinion that I suffered from dyslexia; and I also had problems being bullied by a big boy, older than me, who tried every playtime to lift me over the railings, which formed the playground boundary, which backed onto the river. The river could be quite deep at certain times, and it became a real trauma going to school. There were no playground ladies in those days and he was two years older than I was. It seemed to me to be an obsession, and perhaps the only entertainment he had. Anyway, my mother nagged my Dad to tell him off, which he did eventually, and things improved slowly, but it had been hell for twelve months!

Little did I know, but my life was to get far worse!

At six years old, I was taking a great interest in farming, and Dad was certainly encouraging it. Because we lived over a very old bridge, with a few houses nearby, it was decided that because of the condition of the bridge, we were to miss out on electricity for the time being. However, everyone over the bridge had to have an overhead supply. But, after my father died in November, in the second week in December 1952 electricity came to us! In the meantime, it meant oil lamps in the farmhouse, storm lamps in the shippens, and when you went to feed the horses etc., you carried the lamp with you. They were lamps with a round glass which stopped the flame from blowing out which, unfortunately, they did quite often.

I very much remember the big oil lamp in the middle of the kitchen table with my parents trying to read the newspaper. I must mention about the kitchen/living room with its big blackleaded open fireplace in which we cooked and which kept us warm (the picture of one on the front cover of this book is similar). There was no heating elsewhere in the house, so in winter firebricks were placed in the side oven of the large farm kitchen fireplace. Those bricks had got quite hot by bedtime; they were so hot you had to be careful how you got them out of the oven. You wrapped them in a piece of old blanket and you took them upstairs to bed with you, and they more or less kept warm all night, although I think Mum and Dad got the hot water bottle!

With not having electricity, it meant my father and workman milked cows with a petrol engine similar to a generator, which meant some mornings it would not start, and was then taken apart (probably got flooded). So they had to be milked by hand, and if the milk wagon called, and you were not ready with your kits of milk to be collected, he had to come back later and was not best pleased. If I was at home (say at weekends) I would begin my working life by sitting on a little three-legged stool, and drawing the milk with a clean bucket between my little legs. Now the cows were used to this way then, although they wouldn't be today, and they had this nasty habit of swishing their tails (I suppose because of flies and so forth) or standing on one of your feet. It happened one day, and there was no one there so I had to scream for ages for someone to help me move the cow's leg.

For some reason my father seemed to develop a double-edged

personality, in that to his peer group he was the most dynamic, go-ahead farmer and leading figure of the local football club (Croston), though with being slightly lame he could not play. For a period they played on his/our land in Carr Lane. He also was a keen supporter of Preston North End, and with being one of the first to own a car, always took a car full of men to see them play. He became a leading committee man on the local agricultural show at Rufford, looking after the cattle section. In later life, show work was to nearly take over my own life, so it must be in the genes (which I will deal with later), but as young as I was, I noticed he was becoming increasingly short-tempered. In the space of a few years, two workmen left (no doubt because of his temper) and, my God, when they gave their notice in (which seemed to be always on a Saturday morning, witnessed by all us children), he would let rip at them, calling them all the names under the sun. It's surprising they didn't fight him, but I suppose, due to his size, they didn't dare. We even had a Mrs Allen coming to the farm to tell him off for being awful to her husband, probably because she would have to meet my mother in the village most days as well. It did later make me think he perhaps could not stand Dad's temper.

Every year we usually had half a dozen Irish men who would come over to the mainland seeking work. They stopped at some wooden hostels in Euxton, near to Chorley, under the Ministry of Work Department, who would bring them out in sheeted wagons, drop them out at farms that had requested help, and then pick them up at night. In years gone by they used to sleep in the building, cook their own breakfast on a fire, plus their tea, which I was told would be potatoes thrown in the large pot in boiling water which sounded quite good. Fried eggs were cooked on their shiny shovels that they had been using all day, and would really be quite enjoyable in those days. It smelt really appetising!

Other farmers used war prisoners, but we were not large enough to employ them.

My father's mother, my grandmother, had of course remained at the farm since Grandad George had died in 1942, but she had been getting under Dad and Mum's feet, although she did help with the cooking. At this point I must mention that she was an expert in rare dishes, some of which I never remembered eating myself. She used to make sparrow pie. My, there must have been a lot to be able to catch so many. Nowadays, you are lucky to see ten a day! Another recipe of hers was young nettles, cooked in a pan like cabbage, which, of course, are full of iron and which I have eaten—quite good!

As we were on a tenanted farm, we were obliged to let the gentry shoot over the land. We were sent a brace of pheasants, rabbits, partridge or hares, and enjoyed them, but, my God, when my grandmother dressed the hares (with them being hung for a few days), the smell was awful; it went right through the farm house!

She was a very strong, domineering sort of person, and I don't think her sons' and daughters' offspring living now will disagree; and, indeed, all her sons, apart from my Dad, were made to go out and seek their fortune at thirteen to fourteen with only the clothes on their backs, other than Uncle Albert who went to Canada, perhaps to pan for gold, but ended up in a place where it was so cold that when he had a wee, it froze before it hit the ground! Uncle Albert didn't find any gold so consequently came back and went farm labouring, and later worked for the local council. I liked Uncle Albert a lot and he lived near us all his life. Whilst talking about him, I would just like to mention a truly significant day. I had just passed my driving test, and his son asked if I would bring him out of Wrightington Hospital where he had been for what seemed a very long time, and his joy on seeing the green fields was overwhelming and something that I have never forgotten. It was sometime later that I had to carry him at his funeral.

To return to my grandmother, it's true to say, I would think, that we all have got her determination to work and get on in life. Father and mother always liked a circus, and unfortunately we all had whooping cough. If you have never been ill with it then you do not realise how your throat tightens up and you cannot breathe, so we all missed the circus and stayed with Grandma. Monica was very ill and for the first time ever,

Grandma got very worried, and kept waiting at the farm gate for them to get home.

In 1950 an almshouse became available in Croston St. Michael's Terrace, and with prompting from Mum and Dad, Grandmother moved out to go to the almshouse. It was quite funny really in that she was made such a fuss of by the Methodist people at the chapel just across the road that she became a regular chapel-goer, even though she was C of E and had never had a good word for them before!

J. Perry, 66, Lytham Road, Fulwood.

Family clan with our icon, Grandma Whalley (5th from left) together with Mum and Dad (3rd and 2nd from left)

GETTING BACK TO MY LIFE

Photo of Whalley family, 1951 (me on right)

My father's attitude seemed to be all over the place; one minute he was as nice as pie, then next he was laying the law down. We three children were made to wash eggs at the kitchen table for them to be sent away. Monica had now arrived so it was two boys and two girls. Nancy and I were very close, and have remained so to this day.

A man called Albert had started to work for us: he had come from the Ministry of Work. Everyone was quite impressed at the beginning, which would not last forever! Anyway, he was to live in the farmhouse which meant more work for Mum.

I am not quite sure of the date, but Dad got tonsillitis, and with there not being many antibiotics about, he was troubled by his tonsils quite often. It was decided by Mr Anderson (Consultant) that he should have them out. I think Mr Anderson and Dr Rogers were pals. With Father's build being about fourteen stone, his tonsils would be accordingly large, and he was very poorly then and for some time after. Good job we had taken a new workman on!

I must not forget that after school we played with Lawrence Bamford next door, whose family were farmers and corn-threshing people, and who had a steam tractor engine which was not used. We spent many hours just turning the steering wheel and knobs, etc. Later it was scrapped but would have made them a fortune these days! A real 'Fred Dibnah'-type machine.

The whole little hamlet was overwhelmed one day when Lawrence's brother went missing and was suspected of falling into the nearby river. I remember it like yesterday and, of course, it did indeed turn out to be true. It seemed to cast a shadow over the thirty people who lived close by in the twelve properties which included three farmhouses and buildings. It was so tight that one only needed to walk twenty-five paces and you were at that property's front door: a real hamlet!

Being the oldest son, more was expected of me; and yes, for a Christmas present my father got the local joiners to make me a barrow, and my Mum's dad, who had now married Old Alice, as she was known (she had been his housekeeper though she was younger than him), would get me some clogs. Grandad Royle was such a big character in all ways and would often pick us kids up and take us to the next village on his pony and trap. He was an expert on shire horses and he would never have believed that I was to become a shire horse breeder.

School was, I am afraid, not my forte in life. I found difficulty with spelling which I suppose today people would say was dyslexia. We, as children, were all very shy; quite a lot of children were the same and, let's face it, the teachers at that time were hard to please and seemed to shout a lot. My brother, Edwin, went at four and a half for his first half-day and just would not go again until he was five years old. So every day Miss Turner would want to know where he was. It led to me being frightened of Miss Turner asking where he was all the time.

I would be home from school at 3.30 p.m., and more often than not, with most of the arable land being at least a mile from our farm, I was made to walk/run with two lots of bagging for my Dad and workman, onto 'the moss', and woe betide me if I was late. If the weather was nice, I would spend a few minutes in a small tunnel under the railway track, and it was quite an experience when it shuddered when a long train went over it. I was to think later on in life that I would get there for 3.50 p.m. and Dad would be back home at 4.45 p.m. to milk. I think someone was making a fool of me, as I was regularly to tell Mum later in life.

One Saturday morning there was some excitement in the farmyard. At about 8.00 a.m. there seemed to be two people in our haystack, which was part-used and covered with loose hay. Dad reckoned he didn't like the idea of sticking the hay fork in them in case there were two big men there who would hit him. Anyway, he rang the police, who sent a policeman in an MG red sports car; not a bit like the cars of today. He went to the haystack and was soon back to report. We were watching from the bedroom window, having only just got up. It was freezing cold, and we gasped as a bare woman sat up with no clothes on, bold as brass, and got dressed, followed by the male. It seemed that they had missed the last bus home to Liverpool after visiting the local pubs, and for years after I had nightmares. I suppose it was because they would have been mucking around the farm whilst we were in bed.

Farm life carried on as normal. Mr Whittle killed a pig; what a noise! We hadn't had a shire horse for some years, but Dad knew where there was a quiet grey horse at Hundred End, a village five miles from where we lived, and so he bought it. The man who sold it got me and Edwin to walk under its belly to prove that it was quiet and, sure enough, it did its job well. I used to spend a lot of time stroking it at the gate, and many times climbed to the top of the gate and put one leg on the horse's back, scared to sit on it properly, and then it would move away and I quickly got my leg back.

At seven years old, it was my job to get sticks and coal in now that my grandmother had moved out; a job that I have been doing ever since! I've grown up to be a good lighter of fires and still have a bonfire every

November, and a special one at that, but I'm not too bothered about the fireworks.

Monica was growing, and work was being pushed onto my sister Nancy and me: potato picking, feeding hens, washing eggs, feeding calves and mucking cows out. In those days they faced head on so we could safely walk down the centre and feed them. It was still semi-dark and in the winter we were still using storm lamps, and yet the rest of the village was glowing in light through electricity.

My father's moods were becoming more aggressive. Of course, at my young age, I was not aware that migraine was so awful, but the rows seemed to be more frightening and he was always threatening to take his belt off. He used to stop the car and smack us all, and truthfully we were only doing things that normal kids do, although I seemed to be a chatter-box!

There were four terrible instances of beatings that I received. One, at 7 years old, was because I had forgotten to feed the calves. It was winter, and cold dark days, and Dad had been out doing a part-time job for the Ministry of Agriculture, in which he went go round to farms in the district and checking the young bullocks/calves to make sure they were ok, they also had to have their teeth examined for correct age. If father passed them, which he did by cutting a 'V' out of their ear, they got money from the government. Like now, probably the workman was off or we were between staff. Anyway, he took his belt off and kept hitting me, with my dear Mum shouting at him to stop. I remember she grabbed the large kitchen knife and forced her way between us; me in the corner, with the knife pointing to his throat and, thank God, he backed off. I really do think she would have done it. There was more of this sort of thing, the shouting at us, be it to the workmen, delivery men or to me.

It was to be a terrible year in 1952. It seemed to be the usual cold winter, but Dad was to branch out with a big cabin, eighty feet long and twenty feet wide, built by our good local joiner firm, Coxhead and Bretherton. Brian Coxhead, who I know well to this day, worked on it. I remember it well, with other farmers calling to view it, especially with new shavings provided by Coxhead and Bretherton. The chicks duly arrived from Thornbers, courtesy of British Rail, to Croston railway station, and what a picture the chicks looked. My God, we really thought we were expanding! But Dad seemed to have more bad tempers and the migraines were getting nearer together. The next thing was that his eggs were getting more rejections from the people who tested them at what was Preston Farmers Limited, so the rep, Mr Strickland, arranged for Dad to bring his own boxes of eggs, which were in trays of course. They had been washed by us three children.

He handed over his boxes of eggs; I suppose about forty-eight dozen, which seemed a lot in those days, but eggs were about three shillings (fifteen pence) a dozen, and small farmers (with about six acres of land, ten cabins full of hens, ten calves, four pigs, a few potatoes and veg) could make a decent living, self-providing for their own family. Quite a few owned their own property and, maybe in return, could help a bigger farmer to get his hay and harvest in; taking payment in kind so that he would get enough hay to see him over the winter. Oh, for those days to come back, without the war, of course, I think!

Getting back to Dad, it must have been holiday time because, probably to let Mum have a bit of peace, we all would squeeze in the quite large Vauxhall car (black with doors that were hinged what you would call now *back-to-front*, and where the indicators sprung up and out almost six inches). Whilst there were a few cars about, a lot of the cars were bad at starting in winters, through flooding of the plugs, and ours was just like the rest!

Anyhow, my father set off with us with the view that he was going to sort them out and no way was he going to have some of his eggs rejected (which meant that his cheque would also be reduced). But guess what! The bosses elected an attractive blonde-haired processor for him, and Dad immediately was won over. And, of course, there were about twelve that she found under the lamp (which all those ladies used) which either were cracked or had a spot in the egg. I think they were used in confectionery, but we got no payment for them. He came home like a wimp. The girl had certainly used her charm on him and never again was he to question the egg sorters!

I was now in 1952, eight years old, really having to work quite hard; and I knew of other farming lads who were also made to do the same, but we were expanding at a fast rate. I was nearly doing the work of a teenager and my schooling was going nowhere. Dad's temper was getting worse! (Plus Mum was expecting again, though we did not know till later.)

One of my worst memories of what was to be a horrible year was one of the last matches of the 1952–53 football season for Preston North End. One Saturday, Dad took his four mates to watch them play, and as he knew it would be late when he got back he put the food in buckets for his new pullets (young hens), mature hens and calves. He would sort the cows out when he was home to milk them.

As the day went on, I did the feeding. He then came home, changed into his work clothes, went out, and next thing he was back playing merry hell. He took his belt off and started striking out at me. I huddled under the big farmhouse table to save myself. He was striking away, trying to hit me, and managing to when his belt wasn't catching one of the table chairs. For some reason, my grandmother had called at our farm (she probably still thought it was hers), no doubt to pick up some vegetables and eggs, and I was led to believe that Dad gave her a small amount of money to top up her weekly pension. She saw what was going on and demanded, as did my mother, that he stop, but this was to no avail. As I was now eight, I had to do something quickly; and I saw that he had not shut the back farmhouse door, so as quick as a mouse, I ran from under the table with Dad chasing me—he was damn near going to put me in hospital. As our back door was part of our kitchen, the door faced the path leading to our outdoor earthen toilet, down a pathway lined by two tall privet hedges (there was, of course, no toilet in the house; we had to use the push-under-the-bed chamber pot). I ran into the toilet which was about six foot by four foot. It was not long, before I could get the door shut, that he forced it open and laid into me with the belt, with me turning my back to him to save my face. Can you imagine me being forced to lean over the wooden platform seat, which had a special hole to fit your bum? As I said, what a good job Dad's

22

mother and my Mum were there as they both managed to grab his arms to restrain him, and boy, didn't they both tell him off. Today the police would have been brought in, and to this day, I have never forgiven him for being so cruel to me, and all because I was the eldest lad and had mistakenly given the wrong food to the hens and pullets, and some of it was still left in the hens' troughs for him to see. My Mum didn't speak to him for a week because of it, and he was never to hit me again, but his temper was still to remain, although not for very long; and yet I never saw him strike my mother, but there were many shouting matches and she could hold her own.

Winter of 1952 came along. Summer had been very wet and hay was hard to get. After harvest in September, then came October school holidays. Dad decided that we would not employ the Irish lads for potato picking, as we the children could do it. Looking back, it probably meant he would save a lot of money in wages! We're back again to Nancy and me being the oldest and strongest, having to more than pull our weight. With little brother Edwin, Mother and the workman, we did get a good week of weather, which was unusual, and more or less finished the picking of potatoes. By October 1952, and in one of Dad's better spells, we were promised three new small bikes for Nancy, me and Edwin for Christmas, from local cycle man Tommy Dalton. By the third week of October, Dad took to his bed with what seems to be a very bad cold. Everyone blamed it on loading mangles in the cold from a hog on 'the moss' into a horse-drawn tip cart, to be brought home for the cows to eat. Grandmother came to help Mother, with the workman doing the milking, but he wasn't used to animals (Dad must have been very ill to let him do it) and Mum hoped it wouldn't be too long before he was up again. Dr Alexander Rogers came every day, and we were kept away from Dad, no doubt to let him rest. Then one late afternoon, near tea-time (I think it was a Friday), Dr Rogers came with the specialist, Mr Anderson. By this time, Dad's mum was staying, and my shocked dear Mum and we children waited, huddled in the best room by the bottom of the stairway leading to the front door (which was ajar), while Dr Rogers took Mr Anderson upstairs. Fifteen minutes later, they both came back down, and Mr Anderson left Dr Rogers. Dr Rogers spoke to my Mum which seemed to take ages, and we were not old enough to understand what was being said, but there was to be an ambulance sent, and the last we ever saw of Dad alive was when Granny and our Mum stood and watched as the ambulance man, due to Dad's weight, struggled with the stretcher down the stairs. As they passed us at the bottom of the stairs, he never moved. Looking back now, he probably was too ill and they may have sedated him. Obviously, my mother had been up to see him, to get his things ready for going to hospital but Nancy and I knew that for a young and strongly built farmer, something was terribly wrong.

That day, my whole life was to turn around and make me grown up; I had to be! As our dear old Dr Rogers was many years later to say: "Geoff, you never had a childhood." Not until I met my wife, Anne, at twenty years were things to improve, and even then, life had many setbacks to come!

While Mum went every night (as that was the rule: 7.30–8.00 p.m.) to Preston Royal Infirmary (there is a new one now), Aunty Ethel (Uncle Albert's wife) came to help. She suffered from a blood disorder and mid-life crisis, but she became a rock to Mum in those days, going with her to hospital every day and helping with the housework.

Dad died on 5th November 1952 (I don't think we got any fireworks that year!) aged thirty-nine, and I think it was a Saturday morning. He died of broncho-pneumonia, and I remember Mum crying all day and night and for many days after. I suppose she was never to have thought that this would happen. All the village people kept calling to say how shocked they were, and I was to start the job, at eight years old, of being a provider and a father to the family and mother Marjorie. How that woman didn't deserve this to happen to her and all the toil it would take out of her! She was to die such a terrible death, thirty-eight years on, and yet was such an inspiration to us all and to all her grandchildren and friends.

I have called this book *Sticks And Coal* as, from the day my father took ill, I have taken charge, every day more or less, of either cutting sticks, putting them at the side with coal in a bucket ready for the fire being lit or making and lighting it; and when I left home, making sure Mum had everything ready. Forty years later, I was to do the sticks for Dr Rogers as he became frail.

My first duties were to help the workman collect eggs, feed hens every day after school, and go on mother's old bike to the moss to count the young cattle (seventeen, if memory serves me right).

On the Monday morning after my father died, Mr Bretherton (the undertaker) came on his bike to see Mum. I remember it like yesterday. She sat on the left of the black-leaded fireplace; Mr Bretherton on the right. I've never forgotten he was dressed in his clean bib and brace overalls. He was a good man. I think Monica was on Mum's knee, and Mum was crying as she spoke with him, and we three children just sat watching, not really understanding all that was going on. We were to find out later that Mum was expecting Martin. What a sad week that was, with what appeared to be most of the village calling to say how sorry they were.

I must mention Mr Billy Hough of Rectory Farm, Croston, who said to Mum she had not to worry about the farm, and that he and his sons, John, Richard and Derek, would help all they could so that I could be helped to take over the running of the farm with the workman.

It had rained all summer of 1952, and 1953 was to be worse. People will recall the Coronation of Queen Elizabeth II and Prince Philip was held in pouring rain. Mr Hough came on Christmas Eve with a big toy for us all and he was to do that every year (for twenty years or so) till he could hardly walk to our little cottage. He was, as his family are still today, good Christian folk who, together with the Dandy family, were remarkable good friends to my mother and us, and later I was to bury some of the older ones. I have never forgotten their kindness and they always called my Mum Mrs Whalley. They were later to keep telling her what a good job she had done bringing us up.

An important visitor came a few days later: the squire, our landlord, who wanted my Mum to stop on at the farm, and he generously offered to forego the rent for two years. Hell, I was only eight years and three months, yet with a better workman I could have done it. Those offers of kindness were to help to lift Mum's outlook in the following weeks and months.

In a little tin she was to keep all the letters of sympathy she received till six months before her death when, unbeknown to us, she destroyed them. I suppose she knew her life was coming to a close.

At my grandmother's insistence we older children were encouraged to see Dad in his coffin, and his face was very red. It would seem unreal these days for a fit man of thirty-nine to die of broncho-pneumonia. I was always told his illness was in his head, and hoped my beatings stemmed from that, or I would have had all the stuffing knocked out of me.

One of the most important decisions of my life happened to me when we watched the cortege set off from the farm with Dad's coffin carried on the large bier which used to be stored in the church nearby. We were so near the church that everyone walked. We watched through the windows of Mr and Mrs Cottam (an old couple who lived at the side of us across the lane) who had kindly offered to look after us for Mum while the funeral took place and, I suppose, people had something to eat. I was to remember every detail of that day and, even then, I knew I would never be a farmer, but wanted to be an undertaker. I suppose I took more interest when I heard other people had died, and so, indeed, it was to happen; which does seem hard to believe, but I was a deep thinker even at such an early age, and yet at twenty-four could not wait to get back into farming. It's very strange.

One of Dad's brothers, Uncle Arthur from Anderton (which is near Northwich in Cheshire), offered to help Mum to come to a decision regarding what to do with the farm. He was one of Dad's four brothers who all had their own farms. If truth be known, he got in before the others offered, which they did. He had been a town councillor and mayor. You could say he was an organiser, but he still had that 'Whalley' temper, and he too was hard on his children until, I believe, one of them, in his late teens, stood up to him and he then backed off. So, together with his wife, Aunty Mary, who was good at sorting forms out, they made many visits to help Mum plan ahead.

A few days after the funeral, other family members on Mum's side of the family started to give advice, and a most unfair decision was made to cancel the three new small bikes that had been ordered with Tommy Dalton (the local cyclist shop) for Nancy, Edwin and me, for Christmas, following our recent back-breaking efforts in picking potatoes before Dad had died. To this day, I cannot believe that mother went along with it, and we never did get the new bikes till we started work. I often used to say to Mum, "Why did you do it as they would only be about £8 each?", so we used old second-hand bikes instead. I remember that I had to use Mum's lady's bike and could not sit on the seat and reach the pedals. She did agree that she should not have done it. The best Mum's side could do was invite me to Mum's brother's (Uncle Jack and Aunty Kitty) for five weeks' holiday! You guessed it—to go and knock muck about and help in harvest! I think the television was the attraction for me there!

A couple of days before Christmas (and you must remember there was no street lighting or electricity in the farm house), at about 8.30 one winter's night, an almighty bang was heard on our back door. The workman was out doing a bit of courting with a mature lady in the village, so mother (with Monica in her arms) went to open the door, and next we hear a big commotion with mother trying to stop what we thought was a tramp taking advantage of her (being newly widowed), and fight she did, until the man revealed who he was: Charlie Ashcroft, who called every day to load the kits of milk on his lorry to take to be bottled. It seems he had pulled his overcoat and collar across his face. His wife was behind him, out of sight, and they had brought a present for us and a tin of biscuits for Mum. They spent, I suppose, an hour with us, saying they were sorry for frightening us all, and do you know, I was to have nightmares for weeks, months and years to come; and when I buried him, I sent him on his way with a bloody good telling-off whilst I screwed the lid down.

Mother didn't have any heart to go and get presents for Christmas, though Grandma Whalley came. I don't recollect her bringing us anything, but Mum's stepmother did get us two pairs of clogs. I should think the girls would not be left out, and so even on Christmas day, I still had my jobs to do, though in autumn we did put eating apples on the floor in the so-called 'best room' so they would be eaten at Christmas time and after. I didn't think in those days about the mice running over them and doing whatever, but they did taste good with the peel taken off.

Winters in those days always seemed to be bitterly cold with frost always on the inside as well as outside of the windows; if only we had had central heating! But work had to be done. Uncle Arthur and mother were becoming concerned that we did not seem to be getting a lot of eggs especially since the hens were not very old. With eggs costing three shillings a dozen (or fifteen pence in today's money), and when men's wages were two pounds, I suppose eggs were then very expensive, and were to go to five shillings (or twenty-five pence a dozen). One had to think if the hens perhaps were short of some vitamins, and our workman, Albert, was no expert; but one day, Uncle Arthur went into the food store and found some nice clean eggs covered with a sack, and right away we knew that the workman was selling them on, so mother knew he had to go. However, Uncle Arthur advised her that, with the farm sale drawing nearer, it would be best (with him living in Cheshire) to make use of him for three or four weeks, and she would then have a good excuse to finish with him, without making an enemy of him.

Anyway, he left us and the district, and that was the last we ever saw of him.

We still had everybody's sympathy and quite a few of the farmers put items in the sale (especially horse implements and harnesses), the money to go to mother. Mother, of course, was now looking for somewhere to live. There were, I think, two council houses up for rent, but although we were young, none of us fancied going in a council house; it really would have been a comedown. The rector in our village came to see mother, and said that he knew of a cottage with land in Out Lane, Croston, belonging to Mr and Mrs Williams. Mum went to see them and agreed £680 which was quite a lot of money in those days, but it was only 400 yards from where we lived and, if I say so myself, the neighbours in that lane knew all about our tragedy and really made us at ease. I will try and acknowledge them here, and if any of their families read this book, it may give them pride that the Whalley family appreciated what they did for us next door and further down the lane:

Mr and Mrs Dick Iddon and Rubin
Mr and Mrs John Iddon
Mr and Mrs Dick and Sally Iddon (no relation to the above)
Mum's special friend: Mrs Frances Smith and husband Jack
Mr and Mrs George Forrest
Mr and Mrs Bill Forrest
Mrs Una Rigby
Mr and Mrs Roy Dickinson
Mr and Mrs Jack Dickinson
(All the above lived in Out Lane.)
Mrs Elizabeth Jackson
Florence Dickinson (dear Florence Dickinson is a lovely lady and is the only one left)
Mr Jim and Nellie Norris (who sold vegetables and sweets and home-made ice-cream)

Frances, Elizabeth and Sally used to share their house with Mum most Saturday nights, and although Mum was twenty years younger, it sort of helped them to have a younger person to (say) walk home from coffee evenings or village activities, and they felt safe. Dad, of course, had not made a will, which meant our assets were not great even after the sale. However, the law stated that mother could only have one third; there was one third for us when we reached twenty-one (I was now eight); and one third was to be invested until she died.

I never knew, even in those days, how the money could go so quickly. It cost £680 for this lovely cottage, and then, of course, we had to pay solicitors. It had no electricity so we had to pay for electrics. Mum's share was then gone.

Mum outside her little cottage

3 Out Lane, Croston

3 Out Lane, Croston - many years later

Once we had bought the cottage, although it did not have electricity, Mum had Mr Bentham do it up for us. It was only a two-up two-down with a wooden cabin as a wash house and an outside toilet. All the gardens were set out lovely, which wasn't to last, but we all felt this was going to be good for us. The front door opened straight into the living room. Mother did not want this small bungalow range, which wasn't unlike the one we had left but not quite as large, and said we would get a tile fireplace when we could afford it, which she did.

By now Mum had had the baby. From time to time you hear of a soldier being killed and leaving a wife expecting, and it being hard for his wife, and it was to be really hard for Mum once again. I understand she was in labour a long time. She said later that she had no energy to get on with it.

The baby was to be called Martin and, my God, he could cry. With Edwin and me sleeping in one room, and in the other, Nancy, Monica, Mum and baby, there was many a night when nobody could get any sleep. It seemed to go on for about three years, with many a smacked bottom, but with no improvement. Mother said he cried for her, but maybe she was not eating the right food; he could have been hungry. But one day he was crying on the living room floor when he heard Matt Taylor's little grey Ferguson tractor going past. He stopped crying, got up on a chair, watched it go by, and then went and got back down on the floor and started to cry again; but it happened that Mum was watching from the kitchen doorway and saw what was happening. I am sorry to say that he got the best hiding of his life and he gave the crying up.

I was now nine, Nancy eleven, Edwin seven, Monica four, and with the baby, money was really tight. Most of our clothes came from jumble sales. Looking back, my clothes did nothing for me. I have never had much flesh on my legs, and I couldn't wait to get someone's cast-off trousers to cover them up. Mother managed to buy two good secondhand cabins, and as eggs were such a good price, she reckoned that it would help to make a little extra. There was one-eighth of an acre to the cottage so for about three years we did fairly well, and I took charge of them. But fowl pest then became rampant in Lancashire and, of course, we (though one of the last) got it. I remember quite clearly the Ministry vets calling on us who had hens to see if we had the virus, which meant slaughter. Because we only had 100 hens, I think ours were taken to someone else's place and either buried or burnt. We did get some compensation and the Ministry workman cleaned our cabins thoroughly.

Mother decided she would not re-stock, and I was getting fed up of cleaning the dropping boards, what with the flies in summer. It was an awful job, and I was quite pleased.

Money was a major concern now as I think she would only be getting about £2 a week, and we had lost about £3 a week income through getting rid of the hens, so she decided to apply for us to get free school lunches, which meant a visit from Mr Smith, a retired bobby who looked after truancy as well as free dinners.

Mr Smith was a very stern man, who showed no sympathy at all with mother's plight, but anyway, the four of us were granted free school dinners; but it was awful at school. When the money was collected, and with us being one of about four families not paying, the other children made fun of us, and for all our school lives my Mum suffered the indignity, about every three months, of him calling unannounced to see if her affairs were the same. Again, I was to bury him later.

About this time, Edwin and I started to take a great interest in football and cricket. Mother's only pleasure was getting the *Daily Mail*, *People on Sunday* and *Lancashire Evening Post* (and I have to say that I read every word of the back three or four pages) and we would fight to get hold of it first.

I have to say I had a very good memory, which is still with me today.

You should not speak badly of the dead, but the headmaster of the local boys school in Croston was a very stern man. He taught all his life at Croston, and had been cruel to parents as well as their children. We were all once waiting for him to wind the school clock high on the wall before assembly, when it fell on his bald head, like Jesus Christ with a wreath of thorns, only his wreath was the clock! Roy Martland dashed forward and lifted it off his head, and he then ran off to the doctors in the village.

There was a lad in our class who was backward, and who was always being thrashed repeatedly by the headmaster for some misdemeanour. He was to end up in a special school. It was sickening to watch. I see him now sometimes, and if he had today's help he would have got by.

I was also there when the headmaster threatened Ann Meadows, and she stood up to him and said if he hit her she would hit him back. That would be about 1954, and would you believe, fifty-five years later I carried out the funeral of her dear brother and one of my best school friends, Billy Meadows. She came back from Australia and she remembered the incident well. The teacher then went on to become a Minister of the Church of England, but not for long—no one would have him. In his place at school came a Mr Lloyd from Chorley, who had a deformed arm, and he really made a fuss of me, and where I normally would not put my hand up to answer questions, I started doing it a lot. It really does show how a different approach can make things happen.

There used to be a man called Leslie Walsh on television, whose memory on sport you could challenge, and Mr Lloyd would ask me some questions on sport and I would usually be able to get it right. He nicknamed me "Leslie Walsh"!

Money really was tight. Mother had to go out to work cleaning and scrubbing. One of the places was really hard, and then Dr Rogers got her to work for him and his wife as well. Also, we had a relative who made cane shopping baskets (not the frame, but the infills), so Mum said she would learn, and so did I. She found it difficult but I enjoyed it. Mr Holmes, from near Wigan, brought them in his van to people's houses. We finished them and he collected them, and for about three years I did them at night. It took me twenty minutes to do one. I would do about twenty per week and get eight shillings for each. I put the cane in the old bath with about six inches deep of water which softened it up, and sat at the back of the living room threading these eight-foot lengths of cane, trying not to hit anyone as I made the baskets. They were flat-bottomed like the baskets girls use for cookery lessons.

Nancy was to do Saturday work in a local shop, and Edwin delivered milk with Tom Taylor. As Nancy was older, she would probably keep most of her money, but Edwin and I would let Mum have half of what we made. I was quite good with my hands and could knit and make rag rugs.

We were now getting overgrown in our little cottage so Martin moved into the lads' room, and for a short spell I slept with my head at the foot of the bed. Then somebody must have given Mum an old single bed and I moved to that at the other end of the bedroom. Sister Nancy moved school to Worden Secondary Modern, Leyland. Croston's Bishop Rawsthorn's Secondary should have been ready for my age group but it wasn't, so mother thought I should go to Worden too. I missed the first year so I was put in the middle tier, but I was hopelessly out of my depth and had never been out of Croston much. Whilst the school was firm, and run with an iron fist by Mr Moffat (due to the large council estates being built around Leyland), in the exams I finished near the bottom, apart from coming top in ironwork and second in woodwork, and being fairly good in sport and history.

MY TEENAGE YEARS

I was now twelve and sports mad, which helped keep me from giving up with my studies.

Mother was so tired when she got home and all of us thought the same. I still got the sticks and coal in, lit the fire, looked after Martin, took him on the bike to get his hair cut and other things like that. Edwin would always do his own thing, but he now became head boy in the first year that Bishop Rawsthorn's opened, which was a great feat and mother was so proud, which just shows however poor you are, if you are clean and have good manners you can succeed in life.

With being one of the last to have T.V., we played out under two street lights. In about 1957, the Australian cricket team were playing England when, one Sunday morning, their test opening batsman, Bill Lawry, came to our next-door neighbours, Rubin and John Iddon, to see their pigeons (who were very good ones) and they never told us! That would have made my day! He later was to captain the Australian cricket team.

Mother had decided that we must improve the cottage a little, and found out she could get a grant for a new toilet and brick wall (to separate the wooden wash house) if she would re-plaster some of the walls to hold back the damp. So she employed a real character from our village in Croston, George Iddon, to do the improvements. His family are still good friends, but I don't think they will mind me saying that though he was a good churchgoer, he could be rough (say) mixing cement or plaster on the lino! He was good in that he didn't push for his money. He was to have another good idea, and in lieu of some of the money we owed, mother was to agree that I would use my spare time (be it weekends or holidays) to labour for him. I spent days raking brick joints out, on tall ladders, while he followed pointing them up, and then he made me walk back through the village with a noisy handcart. How I hated that! This went on for two years for no money.

I would in time bury George, and look back and say he was a truly good character of Croston. He also decided to expand and build a shop. "Joe Soap" here had to help him, and Jonathan Jackson, to build it. Next thing, he got permission to put a large army hut at the back of the shop, which was put on a brick base, four feet high. For a week in hot weather, I helped George and Bob Sumner to put this tall sectional wooden building up, and it was awful with me being only a lad. I don't know how we avoided being killed or hurt, but fifty years later, it's still there!

I was now finding school a lot better: still top in metalwork; second in woodwork, mad keen on sport, and also keen on gardening. At school, with it being a new school, the biology teacher, Mrs Sizewell, took it upon herself to set out the main entrance to the school with flowers and plants, and I was to help. I was in my element in that I had been used to digging and recall her stopping everyone else to watch how I dug, which I still do well to this day. I already knew that, with my birthday being the sixteenth of July, I would leave school while still only fourteen years old.

Edwin's boss, Tom Taylor, used to take him and me, and one or two others, to see Tom Finney play at Preston, and we were there when he played his last match against Luton. It is my privilege to write about Tom later in this book.

My form teacher was Les Hocking, who, out of the blue, made me school cricket captain for the first time in my life. I sensed that maybe there were other things to do apart from work! Just imagine me, captain of a large secondary school, where I should meet up with two of the best cricketers, and my younger brother head boy of another large school in Lancashire.

Also about that time, the great Conrad Hunt (West Indies Test opening batsman) came to teach religion at the school. (I think he was still getting cricket experience in what was known as the Lancashire League and he played for Enfield.) He did seem to us to be a really good man, and one day said he would donate a signed autographed bat to the best cricket player. I surely thought that, seeing as I had opened the batting against quite good bowlers from other schools, that I might get it, but he gave it to my opening bowler, Colin Pickup. Conrad did, of course, go on to great things with his batting, and finished up as the British High Commissioner and died in 2007/2008. In those days, West Indians were not always treated with respect, but he was up there with the best.

As you can imagine, it was desperate that I get a good job. Dr Rogers again came into the picture, saying his friend owned "Treasures Antiques" in Preston and could find me a job restoring old furniture, which did appeal. Nancy worked at Leyland Motors and knew someone who could get me a job in the pattern department (to those who don't know, it is making things in wood, from drawings, for engineers). And Mum's sister lived near to Richard Hunt (Joiners), whose brother-in-law, Jack—incidentally, as I write my story—has just died, and in a few days I shall be conducting his funeral.

What appealed about the joinery firm was that they did undertaking (the wish to be involved with funerals had never left me). I did get the job, and I was able to pay weekly to the same Tommy Dalton as previously, to finally get my new bike at long last, although only a cheap one.

In two of the three years at the Leyland school, Mum could never afford an overcoat or mac for me. Whilst I did go on a bus, it was a mile to walk or run when we got off the bus. We also needed to stand at the bus stop both going and coming home. In bad weather, we didn't have any of those fancy jackets with hoods, but with Nancy leaving, I was to use her old coat—only when it was raining—and hopefully no one would realise that the buttons were on the lady's side! I was also to have to use this mac when I went to work on the bike. God, things were difficult!

For someone who had hated school all his life, the last four weeks were grand—no pressure! That school had been the making of me. Never once did I need my mother to intervene. I had somehow come through unscathed. The day before I left the school, the headmaster had us all in his office, one by one, and when it was my turn, he asked if I had a job to go to. I said "yes" and he wished me well. Pity he had never spoken to me before. And he then asked for my prefect badge back. He seemed surprised when I said I had never had one (but said I should have had!). I went on my new bike on the last day, and I took off after my last free dinner, not waiting to be formally discharged, with a feeling (I should imagine) of being freed from a prison camp. What a lovely feeling of freedom!

Whilst at school, I was showing promise at being a joiner, and Mum's friends would ask if I would encase their iron baths in wood. Some were more difficult as they were nine inches off the wall, similar to today's fashion. They were quite hard to do, and I had to cut the corners by hand. It would cost £2 for materials and I would receive £2 but would keep it in a tin for later.

I would also line big garages with cardboard. Night after night I would do this for seven or eight pounds. No fibreglass then, but it kept a little frost out. Grandma used to make me a rice pudding, in lieu of money, to dig and mow her back garden and turn the front garden soil over and help her put in plants. Next door to where we lived there was an old-fashioned telephone exchange, where mother was asked if she wanted to be paid to keep the ground around it tidy. It was horrible land, but she got, I think, £20 a year, and I did my best. It seemed to grow good peas but the potatoes always got eaten by slugs.

Mr Dick Iddon and Bob Tuson, both good and kind men, would invite Nancy, Edwin and me along with others to pick gooseberries. These were long days—9.00 a.m. to 4.30 p.m.—and made your fingers sore. What they weighed made us about £1 or £1. 10 shillings. For three years I also picked potatoes for a local farmer, Matt Taylor: this was done the week before mother's birthday, during the October school holidays. If it kept fine we would expect £4, but it nearly always rained and we were lucky to get £2. 10 shillings. I usually got Mum a pinny (as they were known in those days) or nightie from Bessie Martland, or something else. Bessie would advise me.

I should then have been having two weeks holiday—but not to be! George Iddon came and asked if I could help him wheel some rubbish, bricks and plaster away. It seems mother had got some wallpaper and paint, and it was the one way of paying for them!

The Saturday before I started work, I went to Preston with mother to get fitted out with bib and braces, overalls, work boots, cheap watch, food bag (the khaki type, where straps went over your shoulder and under your arm), and Stanley tools which Mr Hunt said to book to him from R Slingers, Preston, and then pay him back; so I was in debt from the start.

Monday came! I had four miles to cycle to Much Hoole and I began the long learning curve of a joinery apprenticeship for five years. It was a fascinating firm in the variety of work that we undertook. You could be in someone's posh house next day constructing a dutch barn, splicing a window, erecting a block of greenhouses or helping Will Hunt who seemed to make all the coffins, polishing them with beeswax. I would have loved to go out and help to put someone in a coffin, but Richard Hunt and Will seemed to always do it.

It is true to say that when you join what was quite a big firm, you can always find things to grumble about, but some of the men were the very best craftsmen I have come across, and I think they must have liked me because they often asked me to go with them; partly because I was very keen. I learned a lot from Dick Jackson, Will Hunt, Bob Watson, Abel Watkinson, Richard Corless and Sid Wright.

This next paragraph will take some believing in that the lad who started work before me, Daffy Williams, killed someone later and was given life, but was to kill himself in prison. And the lad before him, Tom Sharp, got a prison sentence for grievous bodily harm, and yet they were both good to me. Tom was a really good worker.

The two apprentices after me were also grand lads, but we were now at the start of the craze for long hair and, whether it was bad management or what, both were given a written ultimatum, pinned on a post in the workshop, that if by Monday next they had not been to the barbers, they would be sacked. However, they stood their ground and down the road they went! It then meant that I had to revert to being the tea lad. We used old "singing" kettles on a cast open fire on which we burnt some off-cuts of wood and large shavings—not machine ones, but from hand planes—and if you did not get your water boiling then tea leaves floated on top and they were not best pleased. Oh for electricity!

Tom Brown came next, and in time he was to start his own furniture business and has done very well for himself.

I will come back to my woodworking life later.

When I was sixteen, I got in Croston Cricket second team and played some twenty years, but I only played a few times for the first team which was of a very high standard. I played under two grand captains: Brian Bromley and Colin Ellison. I found it hard to find time to practice when I started my own business.

Mother had retained good friendships with the local gamekeeper, Frank, and his wife, who lived on the moss. They had two children. One was Barbara, who Nancy was friendly with, and Francis. When we moved into the middle of the village, their Sunday papers were delivered to us, and they came and collected them for many years. Francis was very kind to me and taught me to drive. I won't mention their surnames, but just say that a few years previously (probably five years since Frank's wife had died), he had taken a fancy to Mum and many a time dropped hints that they should get together. But while Mum had a lot of time for their family, she was not going to get involved with a man who was set in his ways and was probably about fifteen years older. I think she thought us children would find it hard to adjust and, while I never said anything, I went to bed thinking (and perhaps Nancy did as well) that I was going to be unable to adjust to a man coming in and taking over. Financially it would have made a big difference to our lives, but at what cost to us? So mother didn't encourage him. I was later to do the funerals of Frank and Barbara, and still think a lot of them both and their families.

I can honestly say that I could think of only one thing when I started work: that I must have some transport. I was cycling everywhere, and Mum was struggling to keep a roof over us, although it was nice to get a cheque for £20 twice a year from General Electricity from the money invested in guaranteed stock. Uncle Arthur would visit us about four times a year and leave £20 each time—in those days it really was a good lift and must be worth about £80 in today's money. Mother's father had died by now and Old Alice was to get her revenge for her not being accepted by the family by taking his funeral service and burial to Burscough, a fairly large village. Grandad's family sat at the back of St. John's Church. We all knew that the farm was not making money and was almost broke. Old Alice got sheltered accommodation in our village, and Mum's two brothers, Len and George, did not take the tenancy on. I must mention that Uncle Harry and Uncle George would take us places and bring food. They were very kind, but lived away.

Twelve months later, Uncle George and Uncle Len were in serious money trouble. Old Alice had never paid their stamp, which every twelve months they were supposed to see and sign. If memory serves me right, Uncle George came begging to mother to see if she could lend them £188. All the money she had in the world must have been only £200. She was to need time to agree, but it seemed that they would be prosecuted so she relented. Whilst it was paid back at £5 a week, it never got put back, so we lost out; and it was to come back and haunt us later with real sadness.

LIFE MOVES ON

Nancy met David Greenwood from Much Hoole and got married at Croston Parish Church. They had, and still have, a good partnership and are blessed with three good sons: Stephen, Ian and Simon, who all have nice families. I often say that David has never altered and has been a good friend to me. They are both well respected in New Longton, which is near where I live. And, of course, it was my pleasure to give Nancy away. Mum went to a good shop for her outfit and looked quite the part. Most people nowadays thought Mum had been left more money than she actually had, and she also used to say to everyone who she met that she was a widow with children (I think to cover the fact that she was poor and maybe to get a little sympathy).

Croston was noted for its large church "walking day" (called Coffee Day) where the Sunday School children all wore white. There was a funfair, and there would always be two shire horses which would pull horse lorries decorated with paper flowers (which the smaller children sat on). Later, as I write this book, I will come back to the horses.

One little amusing incident used to happen every Coffee Day. When the procession arrived at the front of Croston Hall (which was down an unmade little road, over a small bridge, where the procession would be greeted by the squire and his sister). If my memory serves me right, the band would play for them when the Rector of Croston, Richard Rawstorne, would ask my mother if she could spare a minute. He would then ask her to follow him behind a bush where he would give her a ten shilling note. He would do this for the rest of the time he was the Rector. We got to look out for him in later years, making a beeline for Mum, and years later she assured us that no hanky-panky took place—and we believed her! He had been good to my mother and us, helping us get the little cottage, and he knew Mum was helping others in dire straits. There were, after all, no state handouts like there are today, and I suppose the ten-shilling note is worth about £10–£12 today. She would probably spend half of it only so we could have a ride on the fair, and try and get a gold fish.

Just as I think I have nothing more to add to my book, on this day, 24th June 2014, and waiting for the Publisher's editor to finish their work, our local evening newspaper, *Lancashire Evening Post*, in its 'On This Day' feature stated that on the 24th June 1313, at the Battle of Bannockburn, Robert the Bruce defeated Edward II of England, which is the same Rev Francis Bruce's family that I have worked with most of my life–the same family who found a desperate woman (my mother Marjorie Whalley) and her children a little cottage to move into–the same family who used to give mum a ten shilling note behind the rhododendron bushes, and are our dear friends to this day.

One remarkable statistic of that walking day (held the first Saturday in July every year) is that in all my life being involved with it (some fifty years), it has only rained the procession off once, and even then we had set off. People to this day remember it as it rained buckets, and yet it always to used to rain Friday before or Monday following, and still does!

I was later to be involved with the Royal Agricultural Show which is later on in July. The rain always nearly spoils the show, so the motto is: never arrange an outdoor event in July if you can help it, as the weather always seems unsettled.

Going back to my ambition to own a car or van, I continued to work hard—to do work for friends at night and Sundays. We always worked Saturday mornings, and found time for sport most Saturday afternoons.

David Greenwood's dad, Tommy, and his wife, Annie, were good people, and were good to Mum. He found me a van which I put down £100 on, and borrowed the rest, and I was off and ready!

Jim Norris let me park the van in his garage near to where we lived, I was now able to take the van on the road with the help of Francis, who was to help me to learn to drive.

Francis now took me out learning to drive but it was the beginning of one of the worst winters ever: 1963. It hindered the learning-to-drive process, and I also ended up in hospital with acute appendicitis. That diagnosis came about through Dr Rogers because over the past seven or eight years I had had bouts of terrible stomach pain. It usually lasted for about half a day and then it would go. One day, while mother was cleaning, Dr Rogers just happened to mention whether Geoffrey was having any more stomach pains, and she told him about me having had a pain the day before. He told her to send me to see him the next evening in his surgery, which I did, and straight away he placed his hands on my stomach and I flinched terribly in one place. He then said in his Scottish accent, "Hospital for you, my boy, and if you don't, it will burst tonight." I was taken to casualty and operated on that evening, on a full stomach, which was to make me sick later. I think I'd had cabbage and potatoes! I was kept in for fourteen days, in Albert Ward, and it really did seem a long time.

To return to my driving, Jimmy Norris said he would take me to Southport to take my test. There was no synchronisation on the lowest gear and it was only three forward gears and reverse. Of course, I didn't get a very pleasant examiner, and near the end of the test we were coming to a hill, with only a slight incline, and there was a pensioner walking slowly up the hill. The examiner asked me to match his speed. He knew I was gaining on him, so I stopped quickly to get into first gear, and when we finished the test, I was failed for not having control of the gears. I was very disappointed, and tests were being cancelled because of the very bad winter, so it was another four months before I could take it again, and pass second time!

Things were looking up. I was now going to work on four wheels and doing jobs at night as well as days.

Sport also was becoming a large part of my life. I didn't need to go on the Fishwick buses to see Preston North End, and soon got a Ford Anglia car which was green with leather seating, and I washed it every Sunday.

In 1964, with a car full of mates, we went to Oxford to see Preston win. I am not sure who we played at home but we got to the semi-finals at Villa Park to play Swansea Town. The M6 motorway only went to Cannock in those days, but before we got to the end we landed in a big traffic jam. It was pouring down with rain, stop-start, stop-start. We finally arrived five minutes after the game had started so for very nearly all of the first half it was hard to see anything as, of course, we had to stand up behind people who were already standing up at the back of the terraces. But what was to happen now was incredible in that Tony Singleton, our old-fashioned centre half, had spotted Noel Dwyer, the Swansea goalkeeper, off his goal line, and Tony, from all of fifty yards, let rip, and the ball sailed over the goalkeeper's head and we held out to win. So off we were, going to Wembley!

We went to Watford, got the Tube, and enjoyed every minute. What with the World Cup being held in England, and winning it, and meeting up with Anne, the love of my life, things were really turning out for the better.

Also, all the big groups such as The Beatles, The Rolling Stones, Cliff Richard, Gerry and The Pacemakers, Connie Francis, Jim Reeves, The Searchers and Roy Orbison were appearing at Preston, Blackpool, Southport and Wigan. What an exciting time!

Now that I was with wheels, I was probably amongst one of the first of my peer group to own their own vehicle.

I was now dating a lovely young girl called Anne, and she and her mother introduced me to the Methodist Church and we have been involved ever since. We married at Hoole Methodist Church (which is now next door to where we live) and are trustees/members. We were married by the Revd Kenneth Bounds. I say 'lovely' a lot, but he and his wife were lovely to us.

At this stage I must mention that with help from Anne's mum with the deposit, we were able to buy our first home for £1300 at auction. That was an experience! The semi-detached needed modernising which, thankfully, I could do mostly by myself.

It was there, twelve months later, that our first daughter arrived—

Janice—and who, forty years later, is helping me with this draft.

By now I had been promoted to driving the wagon, and as Mr Hunt had moved, we did not always see him first thing in the morning. This particular morning, two of the workmen and myself looked at the diesel gauge and felt that there was enough in it to get us to the place where we were going, and back. Unfortunately, on the way back, at the top of a bridge, the diesel must have run to the back of the tank, and the engine stalled. I knew it had to be bled, but did not know what to do, so we had to get a local garage to get us going and bring five gallons of fuel. The boss didn't say anything next day when I told him, but a few days later, on a Saturday morning, he came to me and blew his top as the garage man had charged a £5 call-out fee which was twice as expensive as it should have been (these days £5 would be £60). I was that mad because I knew I was saving him many pounds in being able to drive the lorry and stop and work with the men. So, being how I am, I went home and managed to rake up £5 in notes and coins and went back and threw it at him, and told him that I hoped it would keep the bloody firm going. Half an hour later, he came back and just said he had wanted a bit more consideration of my duties, but I had done nothing wrong as we always had to ask him first if we could go and get fuel. So I just said, "Get my cards, I'm going". I had totally forgotten that Anne was to give up her job to have our first child that Saturday! As I went through the gates to go home, fully laden with all of my tools, a young lad shouted at me, saying, "Mister, your shoe laces are undone." It was, of course, 1st April (April Fools Day). He does not know how near he was to me killing him!

Having walked out on my employer, I needed to find work. With mother having the land and empty cabins, I set up as a joiner in the village, where I was well known. I knew that Walter Ashcroft Produce Merchants, Vegetable Growers and Animal Feed Supplies (which, incidentally, forty-five years later still supply me) wanted their big Dutch barn wirebrushing and painting. So they got the paint and I did it off a ladder (not scaffolding then). I did a few other jobs and helped them to cut cauliflowers, but unfortunately I became ill. Doctors were never sure what was wrong with me, but I was to suffer in the months of June, July and August with asthma and hay fever. It took twelve years before I moved to Dr Sarah Lewis of New Longton (who is a fine doctor) and it was soon sorted with pills and inhalers for which I am eternally grateful.

A most important development occurred in the lives of both Anne and myself. I was working on Humphrey Moon's house in Croston when I happened to mention to him that I had always dreamed of becoming an undertaker since my father died. Unbeknown to me, that evening he went to the previous retired undertaker, Tom Bretherton, and then called round at my mother's to get her to tell me that Tom would like to see me. The dream was to happen! If you recall, it was Tom who came to Mum's when Dad died fourteen years previously. I spent two evenings being coached in his ways and I and my daughter, Andrea, still do the job just as his firm did forty-five years before, the only difference being embalming and sometimes the dressing of the deceased.

Tom dressed in a plain black good suit plus overcoat, so I went to Orrys on Lord Street in Southport and then put the word about. I was the youngest undertaker who owned his own firm in the country, and it never crossed my mind then, that thirty years later, my daughter would beat my record!

I put plans in for a new workshop and rooms of repose behind my mother's cottage. It was soon passed, and one of my friends, Arthur Heyes, did the block work. Months went by and our second daughter, Alisa, was born—a beautiful girl with blonde hair—but still no one asked me to look after their deceased relatives. I think it was my youth more than being disliked!

And then we got the call! It seemed that it was a lady by the name of Roocroft and she was a relative of the retired undertaker, Tom Bretherton. So I met the relatives, got a bit more coaching, hired the funeral vehicles from Bamfords of Eccleston (a village near Chorley) which was run by Mr Bamford's son-in-law, Alan Jones, who is to this day a good friend (though he retired a long time ago), and we now had our own fleet of vehicles.

Funerals then started to come slowly; at first one a month, then one a fortnight, one a week, and then we became established.

Most of the deaths happened at home and, until the 1960s, you would normally find when you arrived at the home, that one of the older ladies would already be washing the body. I would just help with the moving and help to hold the deceased while we put the nightie or nightshirt on.

To give the reader a little insight into a profession which, you could say, is clouded in mystery, I will write a little about how we did things in those days.

Firstly, one would wash the body all over with some nice-smelling soap, taking care not to roll them over on their stomachs. If you did, then you would get lung purge, which meant you would get all sorts of matter running out of the mouth and which also meant that there would be much left in the throat and on the mattress.

I always used one of the top sheets to cover the deceased whilst I was washing them. If you turned the sheet from one end, you could retain most of their modesty. When you finished washing, it was nice if you used a little talc. And I would also make a nappy out of a towel.

Mum's friend who helped her with confinement, Kate Wood, often came to stay for a couple of days as she got old, before finding a flat in Southport, and she told me how she did laying-out to retain people's dignity.

After about two years, most of the old ladies had retired and I did everything myself. Most families had a bottom drawer where the lying-out sheets, pillowcases, and night attire were kept. I became, and still am, quite skilled in the presentation of the deceased. I always liked to have a bolster pillow under the head, then two pillows with crocheted edgings. These pillows/cases would be placed either side of the person's head, with a nice white sheet over the deceased neatly turned back just below the chin; and quite often a Bible was placed on top of the sheet under the chin to keep the mouth closed. Then a sheet, similar to a tablecloth, was placed over the top sheet with a white handkerchief over the face and then the person would look much like the Queen! When I had finished, we sometimes put a board on the mattress to help keep stains away and keep them straight—there were many awful mattresses.

We then got the chance to buy Goose Green Farm, with two acres of land. It was very difficult to mortgage, but Mr Davies, the bank manager, came to our rescue again and sent me to a friend of his at the Britannia Building Society, and provided I could wait two months, I could have £8000. With us putting up the rest, and apart from adding more land, we are still here today with the site being involved in four major developments (which I will deal with later)—namely the Country Fair, the Woodland Burial Ground, Shire Horses, and the planning permission granted for a new church on site.

Our next arrival was Michael. As the midwife, Mrs Howarth, was correctly to say, "All these Michaels are usually hard work."

A unique funeral and friendship developed—one of many experiences that I might put in print at a later date—when I did a funeral for Donald McKillop's sister in Mawdesley near Chorley and was asked to take the Ashes back to their Church in Berneray, Outer Hebrides—this small island only having a population of 140 people and was made famous by Selena Scott who interviewed Prince Charles in the very same house that Donald and Gloria owned, me and Anne sleeping in the very same bed that Prince Charles had used! The McKillop family are relatives of Sir Joseph Paxton who designed the Crystal Palace dome at Hyde Park, and I had the pleasure of seeing all his set squares, compasses and measures, etc. Berneray is a fantastic place with golden beaches, good fishing, but they frequently get force 10 gales which I believe is an experience to behold. Do try and visit sometime and visit Mr Forshaw's shop (Mr Forshaw originally coming from just down the road from us in Tarleton, Lancashire).

I was now starting to become a farmer with all this land that I had, but what was pleasing was that the land adjacent to ours was Anne's parents' farm, which meant that we could all just jump over the ditch and walk to each others places. Anne's family had lived a very long time at what was called Manor House Farm, a listed farmhouse with a dried-up moat. We really did feel that things were changing for the better, but it came as quite a shock for Anne and myself that there was another baby on the way, which, of course, was Andrea. We didn't realise then that so much trauma was on its way!

Together with all the difficulties over Andrea, the other children were growing up. Janice went to work, and in time she was to meet Graham Webster, whose family were well liked. His mum and dad are really nice people, and Janice and Graham were to get married in December 1993 (yes, December!). Two years later, they had a son, Christopher, followed later by Jonathan.

I was splicing some windows one day when the ladder slid along the flags and one of my legs and feet (my right one) landed on the ground before the ladder. If you can imagine the metal rung, which is what you stand on, well, that came into play; and as my tibia broke, my ankle joint split upwards like an axe, chopping the bone. I then had to untangle my leg and foot out of the ladder. The lady whose house I was at ran out to help, but I knew it was bad. I got the ambulance; and it really was terrible—it seemed that my leg had gone part way into my ankle/foot. It could only be operated on the day after, but the pain was so bad that an emergency cast was made. The international rugby player, Bill Beaumont, was visiting his dad across the ward, and he came over to speak to me; and in the words of TV commentator Bill McCharen he said, "Y'll nay be fit for Saturday", and the screws are still in my leg to this day. Poor Anne! A run of funerals came in from miles away and she was missing me at home, but she was ever so short-tempered with me and I was really down. I knew that financially we would suffer. Revd David Day, at my bedside, offered me all his life's savings to keep me going. I refused, but he really meant it and I knew he wasn't wealthy.

I put pressure on the doctors to get me home. It should have been four weeks, but they let me go in two weeks. This takes a lot of believing, but that first night at home (in my own bed) a mouse ran over my head! I sat up quick. There were screams everywhere! Anne went first thing next morning to get twenty mousetraps. I set them, and Michael placed them where I said; and within one hour, six went off! We were to kill about twelve and traps were going ping-pong. All this time, at least for eight hours, there must have been a nest full of young ones who decided to go walkabouts.

I was ages in getting right. The physio damaged my ankle through making me put all my weight on it within twenty-one days and it had to be re-set . It took twelve months to walk reasonably, and I can feel it every day now. I have less movement in that leg, but a lot of builders suffer similar breaks—either side of me in casualty, two men had both suffered ladder accidents.

Alisa met a young man called Malcolm, got married, and had a son called David on Christmas Eve. Unfortunately, David was born with Mosaic Syndrome, and later Alisa became seriously ill with an epileptic fit. Out of respect for both her and David I do not wish to go into further details.

Whilst all these incidents I have written about had been hitting us both at regular intervals, I had battled to go about doing my work— many times helping folk with doing repairs rather than making them have new, but we all have to live with our consciences, and like every business in the building trade, we had to carry some slow or bad payers.

I went through a period where quite a lot of funeral accounts were taking about six months to be paid through solicitors, with a few even reaching twelve months. I cannot see why solicitors allow this to happen. There were, and are, three firms who still do business that way. With a third of your turnover being unfairly held back in the knowledge that your total invoice is less than the big firms, you can well understand that, because we undertakers pay up front (and accept every customer at face value), some small firms, similar in size to ourselves, just sell out rather than struggle to keep going, instead of carrying such a large burden of debt.

But it has now improved a little with the banks now able to pay direct if they have a copy of the funeral bill. In the line of debtors we are first to be paid even before the taxman! But we carried twelve very big debts—at least, for us, they were. I just hope that those concerned may one day pay back what we are owed.

Getting back to what was going on around me, Michael, our son, decided that he must join the Royal Navy, so off he went and, being a Whalley, he landed up (at sixteen years ten months) in the Elite 32 Group, where at the passing-out parade he carried a real gun, and went on to be stationed on HMS *Manerva* as it sailed to East Germany at the time of the Berlin Wall coming down. Anne and I were very proud when he stood guard at night with real ammo to resist invaders. But it was not to last! He found it hard to live with twenty men in a confined area, and because he joined before seventeen he was allowed to leave. Some of the other recruits were thirty years old! So he came home, and he went to Bath College and did a two-year course in monumental masonry. We set him up as a monumental mason and he is now one of the best. He has two showrooms now, one of which is near Wigan at the entrance to Gidlow Cemetery.

Anne and I attended every home match at Preston North End, and as season ticket holders we sat near the player's wives. Anne liked a good square-up and she certainly holds her own with me!

The shire horses were now becoming a big part of my life, which I will write about in a later chapter.

Andrea had joined with me to be an undertaker, although she had one small difficulty in that (and I suppose because of her illness) she was only five feet tall. Even at the age of twenty she only looked like she was fifteen and many times clients would ask if she was helping out whilst at school! She is a cracking undertaker—very caring—and now gets special requests to officiate rather than me, so I sometimes just drive the hearse. She is now the superintendant at the burial ground as well as being a partner. We are on a police rota list for removals of sudden or suspicious deaths, murders etc, and she quite likes the importance of arriving in the middle of all the activity. She's quite strong for her size, and sights and smells don't seem to bother her.

ANDREA: HER ILLNESS

When I say that there were fifty children and probably seventy parents, you will guess that it was a big clinic with a large waiting room. From day one, you sensed it was a special place, with the very latest toys, books and learning products, all donated by large firms. This was Alder Hey Children's Hospital, Liverpool.

When Anne and I looked around us, the children didn't seem to be very ill and most were playing as if they were at school. Looking back, with it being summer holidays, maybe some had come with a sister or brother which would create a joyful environment. Anyway, when we looked down at our little lass, all wrapped up in a Preston Royal Infirmary blanket, four and a half months old and weighing nine pounds, too ill to cry or want her milk bottle, we were so very sad and apprehensive.

As the afternoon wore on, of course the numbers went down, and in the course of all this a man came into the clinic and sat across from us. To us, then, it seemed strange that a man would sit in at a children's clinic. You would have thought, if he was a doctor he would have gone straight into the Professor's room and not waited outside; or perhaps we thought he was a rep who knew his place. Finally, it became our turn and we were the last ones. It would now be five o'clock, and if memory serves me right, Professor Jones called him in to sit among us, together with the clinic nurses, so obviously he must have been a doctor—but Anne later said, in a most concerned manner, that he never seemed to take his eyes off Andrea. In what seemed to take ages, they both read out the notes from the Preston Hospital and listened to what we told them, going through every detail, and it was not hard to remember as it was all fresh in both our minds. We ourselves, with support from Dr Sam Moss and retired Dr Alex Rogers, took her to hospital ourselves, but first calling at home with her as we never thought she would make it, and, of course, come back home.

We both watched them look at the X-rays that we had brought, and both seemed to be pointing in the chest area. Then they both examined little Andrea. They were so gentle with her, but I think she was crying with barely enough strength to make her lungs work. In a way, we were saddened and yet hopeful that maybe all was not lost.

Professor Jones turned to us and said he would have her admitted as they could not say with any certainty what was wrong with her. So we followed the clinic nurse down some long corridors until we came onto Ward C2—a large ward with what appeared to be lots of nurses and helpers. We were introduced to a most lovely and (if I may say) good Scouse staff nurse who got a bottle for Andrea and started to feed her. After, I should think, about an ounce of milk, Andrea did not want any more, and in what seemed like an everyday routine to us, the staff nurse pulled a machine (similar in size to a domestic power washer) from under the bed. I think she knew, that we knew, what the next course of action would be, and asked if we would like to go and sit in the lounge area, but we said no, we would stay. She then slid a fairly large suction tube down her throat, turned the machine on, and within two or three minutes, got some mucus up, and took hold of the milk bottle again and gave it to Andrea. What followed was totally amazing in that she drank more or less five ounces in one go, apart from getting wind up. In the previous four months, that had never happened!

Unless you were present, you could not have witnessed the joy that we both as parents felt, that at long last we were getting somewhere. We knew that if Andrea got the milk down and it stayed down, she would start to get stronger and, of course, put the weight back on that she had lost from once being seventeen pounds to now only nine pounds.

I suppose we stayed to about 9.00 p.m., mindful that Janice was only just old enough to look after Alisa and Michael, but that Anne's mum and dad lived only 500 yards away, and that it was a light night.

We had at that time not found the shortcuts so it took about an hour's travel home, some thirty miles away.

I will say it here that our other three children, marshalled by Janice, never once grumbled about the waiting in cars and the inconvenience to them that Andrea's illness caused, but a lot more was to befall on them later on.

It was extremely difficult being a joiner, small-time builder and undertaker as I always liked to call it. With not being too familiar with Liverpool and its roads, both Anne and I liked to set off at 5.00 p.m. which gave me time to do some work, and then we could stay till 9 o'clock in the evening. This went on for a few days; the journey now taking fifty minutes, but we witnessed endless car crashes on the A59 due to its being at its busiest with all the workers leaving for home. I also had the nightmare of negotiating what was called 'switch island' on the outskirts of Liverpool, where it was everyone to himself. It's a lot easier now it has traffic lights. While Anne was, and still is, a good driver, she always felt better with me doing the driving.

In the first few days, things progressed fairly well. I must add that Princess Anne had just had a baby called Zara and we both said she wouldn't have been treated any better than we were. In fact, she was born the very same day as Andrea was admitted to Alder Hey Hospital.

We became conscious of one of the excellent nurses carrying Andrea around a lot when we turned up; sometimes a little earlier if work permitted. Her name was Kitty Mather from around the Knotty Ash district. I don't think she will mind me saying, as this was quite well known, that she liked to go out a lot. I suppose you would say she was popular with everyone and she had taken a liking to Andrea. She used to make her smile, and we became very good friends. It was pleasing to know that when we weren't there, the little lass was being mothered by a grand person. Kitty herself died in 2012 but we were not told till after the funeral.

Our other three children were allowed to visit with us so that kept them in touch with Andrea.

We noticed that after about ten days, they were doing more stringent testing. One was to collect her urine, although she was still making good progress.

One night, Anne and I arrived at about 6.30 p.m., and one of the nurses asked if we could wait till 8.30 p.m. We, of course, would always stay till at least 9 o'clock. Apparently, the doctor who wanted to see us had gone home but she would be getting a taxi back to the hospital to meet up with us later. She duly arrived to tell us that they had found a tumour which seemed to be connected to Andrea's heart. We were both shocked and stunned! In a businesslike frame of mind, I naturally asked if it was cancer and she said they couldn't tell, but they wanted to operate in twelve hours time and that one of the world's leading lady chest surgeons, a Dr Owen, had already been to see her. Dr Owen was not a doctor at Alder Hey, but from Myrtle Street Hospital, Liverpool, which was well known for chest work. I understood that she was the best in the entire country. You can see the concern that the hospital staff showed to the likes of us and other parents—what a place! So sad what happened to them many years later.

Kitty Mather (Andrea's Godmother) with Andrea

The only thing that we both could think of was that Andrea was not baptised. She had never been well enough to go to our Methodist Chapel for a service. The staff nurse said she would ring the Methodist Chapel and ask him to come. She came back to say he was out but that his wife had said he would call in the morning before the operation.

At about 10.30 p.m. that night, as we just sat talking, the phone went, and it was the Methodist chaplain to tell us that the auxiliary nurse, who was our good friend Kitty Mathers, had found a white christening gown-type dress, and had asked two of the big girls (who were about fifteen) to act as witnesses with herself. Kitty was later to tell us how nicely the chaplain had done the service, and I believe they all cried, as I am doing now writing this account. We kept in touch with those two girls for years after.

We weren't Catholics but most of the staff were, and most of them paid for masses for Andrea. What good people they were.

Poor little Andrea, though. She was fighting for her life, but she still seemed to have a sparkle in her eyes and, of course, she was on a life-support machine. We never met the chaplain, but he used to leave his visiting card with a little short message saying that he and Andrea had had a lovely chat! It's hard to believe our own Methodist minister at that time never called, and the chapel was only next door.

Obviously, we kept asking if it was cancer, but all they would say was that they were doing tests and as soon as the results came back they would inform us. If memory serves me right, the operation was on a Wednesday, and on the Friday a message was given to us to ask if we could be at the hospital on Monday at 9.30 a.m. to meet the specialist, a Mr John Martin. We asked the nurses if he was the cancer man, but all they would say was that he didn't normally come on to Ward C2.

Monday came and we were in good time. Naturally, we were very apprehensive and I think we feared the worst. A tall man of about forty-six with a presence about him, came into the ward being followed by what we took to be young doctors/students (about twelve of them). Firstly, he asked if we could just move into the glass-sided lounge for a few minutes, which of course we did. A few minutes later, he introduced himself to us and explained that three days after Andrea was admitted, through traces in her urine, cancer was found, so they had known much longer than we thought. The cancer was extremely rare and known as neuroblastoma, which was a tumour the size of an egg, and which was attached to the underside of her heart. Also, a miracle had happened because that had nothing to do with her feeding problem, which was caused by her main artery crossing her windpipe which had also been stretched when she was operated on.

Anne was crying and I had teared up. I think I kept asking what her chances were. He told us that in all his life he had only heard of four more cases that were similar to Andrea's condition, and that unfortunately only one had lived.

Dr Owen was so sure when she took the tumour out that Andrea was given the first course of a two-year treatment, namely into the open wound; every week for a while, and then every two to three weeks between treatment.

Afterwards, we just went and sat at the side of Andrea's railed, cot-sided bed, with Anne holding her little hands. We didn't know at the time, but she was to suffer so very badly for most of the next sixteen years. By my saying that, I meant she did live through all this.

Kitty told us they didn't normally see Dr John Martin, who was Head of Oncology, in Ward C2, but he had taken the decision after three days that if they had moved Andrea to the cancer ward, then we would have realised immediately the seriousness of what was to unfold, and so, for some time after, we stayed in Ward C2. She was there for some weeks, and then she came home. This was another example of how they cared for us, in that they left us in the environment that we had become accustomed to.

It was still not easy to feed her, but Anne had tremendous patience. and so matters moved on ever so slowly. A cough had now developed, and Anne remembers Dr Sam Moss seeing her in the surgery waiting room at Longton Health Centre, coming in and sitting beside her, and saying that if there was anything that she needed then she must not be scared of ringing him, which was a friendship that was to last and is still ongoing after thirty-odd years.

The treatment, which was horrendous, was by injection into the back of the hand or into the forehead. I had the job of holding her down while one of the house doctors gave the dose. In the short time before Christmas, she had two pneumonia attacks, which required admitting her back to Alder Hey, so, of course, she lost weight and went back to being about twelve pounds.

One of the two pneumonia attacks was to happen two weeks into December. She had been in hospital about ten days, quite ill, when we received a call from the hospital to say that they believed she was fretting and the doctors thought she would be better at home. I had a funeral that day so Anne asked her mother if she would go with her. I don't think there were seatbelts then. So off they went, and three hours later I had just come home from a funeral, and was having a cup of tea at my mother's, from where I worked, when Anne and her mother called. Andrea was still strapped in her seat, but didn't want to stop crying which didn't seem to be right. I told them it would be all right, and I'd follow them home.

Well, it went on and on. I rang my mother up at 10.00 p.m. to ask if she would come if I went to pick her up, so that she could help us. She was good with babies too. We were all sat on our double bed—all the children as well—with this baby screaming, when I said there was something wrong with Andrea's arm. So Anne gets little Andrea out of the all-in-one, which is what the nurses had put her into at the hospital (I suppose, ready for bed), and there, straightaway, you could see the trouble: her arm was broken. The poor little thing. Anne said the way she was crying at the hospital was probably *because* it was broken. It was to be the only thing that we ever could find fault with them about.

I rang through to Ward C2, who put the night sister onto me and who, of course, was very sorry, but asked if we could wait a little while and then take her to the hospital at 8 a.m. There was a full inquiry, and Dr Martin spoke to us from his clinic in the Isle of Man. He referred us to one of his colleagues to set the arm, but, because of Andrea's age, they put two pieces of aluminium at 180 degrees, and bound it with bandages. It would seem that Andrea must have put her arm through the cot sides and another child maybe ran past and flicked it backwards, but why the nurses never picked up on it we will never know. However, this tale gets a lot worse!

We left the hospital at 4.00 p.m. We had been away nine hours and not eaten properly, so we called at Ormskirk, and Anne went to the shop and bought five meat and potato pies, so that it would be an easy tea. Janice was looking after Alisa and Michael who had come home from school. We got home tired, rang the grandparents, and I had my calls to answer, so we put the pies in the oven. By now, believe it or not, Andrea was quite cheerful in one of those baby walkers where the baby's feet just touch the floor. The little girl was moving about in the kitchen; and, would you believe it, a sickly nine-month-old, unbeknown to us, pulled the oven door open and put her little hand in, and burned what was her good hand. There was a big scream and we all dashed to her; and, quick as a flash, we put her burnt hand under the tap. Anne rang Andrea's G.P. who had just gone home, and the phonecall was re-directed to Dr Wilkinson. When we explained the ordeal of the broken arm and the hours that we had been away in Liverpool that day and the previous day, she told us to meet her at the surgery where she was waiting, and she rendered first aid. We have never encouraged our children to be in the kitchen or near fires or run into the road, and yet this happened.

Alder Hey insisted we must go back the following day to let Dr Martin check the break (or, as they are known, "greenstick fractures"), so we took the little girl into the clinic with one arm in a metal sling, and the other arm also now in a sling. We were also still taking her back for treatment. The fractured arm mended in fourteen days, but the burns took months and months to heal. At that time we were really beginning to feel like we were cracking up.

Someone up above must have been keeping an eye on us, and planted (if that is the correct word) the best and most loving Methodist minister: Revd David Day and his wife, Doris Day, who from day one embraced our family as if God were telling him to look after Anne,

Geoff and family, but especially little Andrea. With their love, we were to come through this heartache which in many ways felt like hell. I shall write about David and Doris later.

In order that people reading this book can follow Andrea's progress, I will devote this chapter to covering the early part of her life.

Having got over the broken arm, we struggled on and kept going for treatment every week. The clinic would, I suppose, see about twenty-five patients at each clinic, most coming for check-ups, X-rays and, of course, treatments by injection for the various types of cancer, leukaemia etc. We got to know some of the children and parents by meeting them at the clinic and watching them improve, or seeing them deteriorate ever so slightly over the weeks and months, which meant that some would pass away, while others who were doing well maybe only came to the clinic once every six months. It's hard to believe that we were all enthusiastic about going to the clinic, apart from Andrea.

By now we had got into the following spring, and the poor lass was struggling to continue with the course of treatment but still had fifteen more months to go. We now only went every three weeks, which made things a little better for me regarding work. Funerals had to be over by 1.00 p.m. so that I could take Anne and Andrea to Liverpool. The overdraft was starting to increase, but Mr Davies at the bank was doing all he could to help us.

Andrea was by now back in hospital with a terrible infection and cough. She had no strength to fight the infection and could only make a little whimpering sound. She had something like a quinsy that people used to get before drugs came about. Dr Martin said she should go to Myrtle Street Hospital (which I think is closed now) and have something done to her windpipe (unfortunately, I am not sure of the medical term as it was such a long time ago). So she was taken to Myrtle Street, and that evening we could only go after six o'clock. It was to be the most awful journey—not only were we not sure how to find the hospital (it being right in the city centre), but we were met with obstruction after obstruction, with roads being cordoned off, police at every junction and fire engine sirens going off as they passed us. We were being forced to go round in circles, then came across a sign for the hospital, but couldn't get to it. I parked up in a place where I shouldn't and walked over to a lady policewoman to tell her of our predicament. She was really helpful when I explained the circumstances, and she allowed me to go down a one-way street the wrong way, and she gave us her blessing. She told us that four bombs had been detonated in the centre of Liverpool. One had been in Lime Street Station, the other nearby to where we were, and that the IRA were thought to be responsible. Forty years later I was talking to a man from Liverpool who told me that that very same evening he was buying tickets for a railway journey—of course, he couldn't get his tickets—but he told me there was nothing about this in the papers the day after (it seemed like there had been a news blackout). Really unbelievable!

We finally got there at about 8.30 p.m. and were shown to a little side ward. Everywhere was unnervingly quiet and not a bit like Alder Hey. Anne and I just sat at the side of the bed holding Andrea's little hands—one each. Suddenly the door opened and who should walk in but dear Dr John Martin on his way home from the Isle of Man Clinic! I suppose he would have been just off the ferry boat, but there wouldn't have been many doctors who would have called in late at night just to see how Andrea had got on. We felt greatly honoured and privileged to have known such a man.

Andrea was moved back to Alder Hey next door to recover. As the days went by, she nearly stopped coughing, and she was able to come home, though not for long!

Reverend David Day arranged for Andrea to have a blessing at the Much Hoole Methodist Chapel, seeing that we weren't present at her christening, and it was a lovely occasion.

Andrea had a most terribly traumatic treatment one day at clinic. Dr Martin was not present, and his registrar tried to give Andrea her treatment into the back of her hand. I think every time it was done it damaged the tissue where the needle went in. Two nurses and myself were holding her down on the table. The doctor was struggling and struggling to find a good vein when Andrea, in the middle of all her crying, called out "Daddy, Daddy." That will live with me forever—her first words. The doctor gave up and asked one of the nurses to go and get another doctor as it was distressing him too. The other doctor came and he injected into Andrea's forehead. What a terrible session! Thankfully it never seemed to happen again quite like that.

Sometime later we went down south on holiday to Dorset. Summers always seemed to be wet, and after the children being so understanding about Andrea, we all really needed a break.

We arranged to go to Sherborne Abbey which was quite a journey from where we were staying. We had a lovely time outside and were then given a conducted tour inside the Abbey. We had nearly completed the tour when the lady invited our children (and others) to sit on polished benches around a great oak table where some king had eaten. She gave us the history and the tour then finished. We all got up from the table, but next thing we knew was that Andrea had slipped off the polished bench, and you could see that her arm was broken badly. The staff were very apologetic and rang for an ambulance. The ambulance duly arrived and Anne went in it, with me and the three other children following behind. The difficulty was that we had driven forty miles from our holiday cottage and we were now travelling on another fifty miles further to Yeovil, which meant ninety miles to return to the cottage.

Because of Andrea's complaint, which now looked like she had developed brittle bones, the doctors at Yeovil spoke to Liverpool, and it was decided that she should stay in for the night. We had to leave a crying child and drive back ninety miles to the cottage at 10 o'clock in the evening. We had to do the same the next day and it was really upsetting. The other three children had sat in a hot car for some four or five hours while we had been inside the hospital. We returned to the hospital the next day at twelve noon, and they had put her in a little school. She looked so sad as we looked through the window at her.

Two days later we went on the ferry to Cherbourg thinking it would be a great treat for all the family. I'd never set foot abroad, and they say the world is a small place, for who should be on the boat but Dr Martin and his family. Unbelievable! It never stopped raining all day so adding this to the Sherborne disaster, you will realise what an awful holiday we had.

We returned home and Andrea remained sickly, always having to go back to Alder Hey for treatment and being admitted sometimes. She had a very severe croup (cough) once when we thought that she would not pull through, but she certainly did. The 'chemo' was taking it out of her, and Dr Martin was seriously considering whether she could take the full course. She did lose all her lovely hair, but never lost her smile.

When she was feeling better, Dr Martin said she was 'one in a million' and she was included in the Bob Champion story. People sent her money which we forwarded on to Alder Hey for research.

Unfortunately, when she was about two years old, she fell at home one night and broke her arm. We took her to the new hospital at Preston, but they made an awful job of it so she had to go back to Alder Hey where it was refixed.

My building business was really hard now and we had three or four very demanding customers, and what with inflation running high and bricks hard to get hold of, it was really tough. So a decision was made to cease Andrea's treatment and visit the clinic every month, although many a time she was already resident in a ward.

We just battled on and Andrea seemed to gain a bit of weight by the time she was four, and as we were very good at fundraising we decided to organise a large charity barbecue event for Alder Hey. John Webster brought his hurdy-gurdy-type organ on a large wagon. We arranged entertainment and all our friends supported us. We raised £3,000 for the hospital, and it was a fantastic evening, and John Martin and family attended.

Andrea's mum reminds me that for the first time ever in her life she took an interest about going to playschool which was only next door to where we live. She was treated like a princess, but unfortunately she didn't get to go as much as she would have liked, due to her always having infections.

She started school at four and a half, but was only there a few days when we received a telephone call from school saying that she had fallen and broken her arm. Once more, we were back to hospital, but this time took her straight to Alder Hey. Kitty Mathers had kept in touch with us and so had Sister Randle (who had lost her husband) and who was in charge of the clinic. She was a smashing lass, and she asked me if I could get her son a dairy farming job as he was hoping to go into agriculture (something like DEFRA). He needed some practical experience and I used my contacts to find him a live-in job which worked out well for him.

Without sounding boring, the years went by for Andrea, who still had highs and lows, but we kept her in our bedroom with us until it nearly got embarrassing! She now had her cough back and it really did concern everyone. She had to carry a hankie in her hand all the time to help with the cough. Her mum and I spent hours lying in bed just listening, and many a time thinking whether we should get up and tap her back. We started to think the worst, but the doctors seemed to think that she might grow out of it.

She got to eleven years of age and went to high school but was always sick. I doubt whether she went more than twenty-four months out of four years. Her last year was so bad that we paid a lady called Cath to help her, and she sat her exams at Cath's home. It was no great shock that she didn't do very well!

Anne and I decided, having been invited with Andrea to Dr John Martin's first of a series of farewell dos, that we must see him before he left to discuss Andrea's cough, which we managed to do. He told us that, because she only looked young, he had allowed her to stay in the children's hospital as he had wanted to oversee her progress whilst he was still at Alder Hey. Now that he was leaving, he had spoken to a lady specialist at the Royal Liverpool Hospital who would take over Andrea's case, and he said that he had told her about the persistent cough. We then saw this lady and Andrea was later admitted, but not before she suffered a most horrendous quinsy. Anyone who has had one will know how awful it is. She was admitted to hospital where she had a bronchoscope as an emergency, with the tube stretching her windpipe, and although she took a while to recover, in the past fifteen years she has never really coughed at all. What a godsend!

Rev. David Day, and his wife Doris. A much loved minister at that time

Mother had by now retired from cleaning, but was still going to Dr Rogers' doing his cleaning part-time. I suppose she was like Betty in *Emmerdale*, and would sit and have a cup of tea with the doctor. As the doctor was not terribly well, he used to say, "Geoffrey, I am drowning in my own water" (it being lodged on his lungs) so I used to call with some sticks and see that he had some coal in. Indeed, one night I got him an ambulance as he was very ill. Eventually we got him home, but not for very long. A friend found him dead in bed one Christmas Eve, and I felt privileged to kneel at the side of his bed with his friend Mr Rowley and the Rector of Croston, Francis Bruce, while we said prayers for him. It was a very great loss. I then moved him to my rooms of repose, together with some of his valuables, as he had been robbed two or three times. He left me a stuffed Russian bear that he knew I liked, a grandmother clock, and some other items. At his funeral service memorial I was to read a passage. I again felt very privileged as I don't do public speaking.

Mother used to take it in turns at Christmas to go to different sons' or daughters' houses, usually staying three or four days. With Anne being a good cook, she was always keen to come to us. This particular Christmas, 1989, mother (now seventy-two) had seemed a little quiet, and on Boxing Day had asked Anne not to give her too much to eat as she felt a little unwell. Anne, being Anne, made a special little plate for her with a little bit of everything and Mum seemed to find that grand. She then went home, but two days later was still feeling bloated. She informed us that Dr Marriot, who took over the practice that Dr Rogers used to have (and who was still my doctor), wanted her to go and have a scan. It seems she, unbeknown to us, had indeed been to see her.

With my workshop being behind mother's cottage, Dr Marriot sent a message to me (unbeknown to mother) asking me to call in, which I did. What shocked me was that she insisted I have a cup of tea with her, it being lunchtime. She informed me that the scan results were not clear, and that she was in discussions with Chorley Hospital so that Mum could go into hospital quickly because her stomach was enlarged and might need draining.

Nancy (Geoff's eldest sister) with David

Geoff's mother shortly before she died. She was too unwell to go to the wedding.

She was in hospital a few days when a message was given to me asking if I could see Mr Lythgoe, specialist, that evening. It was arranged with my sister Monica, who was also taking Mum's sister, that they go in first. I would see the doctor and then join them at the bedside with some tale. I waited for the doctor in the ward sister's office, which had a glass partition and through which, if I was careful, I could see mother sat up in bed laughing away to her sister Barbara and to Monica. However, in the next five minutes all our lives were to be turned upside down.

The specialist was to tell me that our Mum had ovarian cancer and that her expectation of life was three weeks. And there she was without what seemed a care in the world.

I was then forced to walk out, down this long-ish ward, and sit down—trying not to let on—with my sister Monica mouthing to me wanting to know what the doctor had said, and hoping that mother wouldn't notice anything. There was mother asking what I was doing visiting that evening as it was not my turn, and I told her some lie about me having to see someone in Chorley. I could tell she didn't believe me, but managed to get Monica to understand that things were serious. All Mum could say was that the lady across the ward was very poorly, and yet that very same lady lived twenty more years.

That hour seemed to be an eternity, but I managed. Outside the ward I was able to tell Monica and Aunty Barbara that she was dying. It's not any easier for me even when I come across death every day. I was shocked that the next morning, I understand they made an incision in Mum's stomach and the water went everywhere. According to my other sister, Nancy, they just told Mum it was all over and there was no hope. What cruel staff they were.

Mum went home to my sister but was given an appointment to see a Dr Clarke (I seem to remember) who came to Preston one day a week from Christies in Manchester. He examined her and said he would like to operate on her. Mum was all for it and I suppose we were too. We had to give her a chance, hoping that it would perhaps give her some extended time as she had no pain.

Come the day of the operation, Monica and I would visit her

when she came out of theatre. It has always been my experience that following an operation, people seem to feel better that day, but worse the following day. When we knew the operation was over, we set off and got there at about 6.30 p.m. We first asked the Sister what the outcome was and she informed us that Dr Clarke had opened the abdomen but could not help her. I think we both had expected that outcome and were ushered into a recovery room. It was frighteningly awful really—she was thrashing about, knocking the cot sides—on her tummy and then on her back—and all the time saying, "I told you not to come". And she kept on repeating these words. For the first time in my life, having dealt with shootings, murders, all sorts of accidents, while I wouldn't say I was a coward (or Monica either), we were so startled that we both left her to come round properly—something I always regretted.

She came home to Monica's and never said anything about the incident. She was given some awful, strong pills which she said made her tongue feel like a knife had sliced it from back to front.

Nancy's son Stephen was at that time getting married to Carole, so Mum was not well enough to go to the wedding, but Mum's friend Nellie Norris stopped with Mum while we all went to the wedding; and later Stephen and Carole, when still dressed for the part, went to see her. What a shame! She was going downhill.

A few weeks later, one Saturday morning when I was in the shoe shop that I then owned, I got a call from Monica asking if I would come quickly. When I got there, Mum was beside herself, rolling about on the floor. I grabbed the duvet and wrapped it round her. I held her for dear life and then she started to have what appeared to be fits every few minutes.

Monica got the doctor (Dr Moss) who ordered an ambulance. The siren was ringing all the way to hospital. We were not allowed to see her for about three hours and were told to go to a certain ward, and there followed another shock—she sat up in a cot-sided bed like a demented soul, thrashing about. She looked me straight in the eye and then lay down. I demanded they give her a side ward so she could have some dignity. She was taken into a side ward where these fits came every hour, but as the days went by they receded. I did the night shift as I didn't need much sleep, and apart from the nurses turning her every twenty minutes, I held her hand all the time. And her hand being so soft and cool, I have to admit I wished her to die: which she did, six days later. It all was so horrible. Poor Mum! She even died Friday evening so she was placed in a fridge. The head mortician, Clare Ingle, would, for me, have left her in the chapel if her death had been in work hours, but it was not meant to be.

I duly registered the death and brought her home to my front room. Canon Brunswick came and said prayers, and she was taken back to her own home on the day of the funeral with the coffin lid off. Martin and I screwed the lid on, and we went to Croston Church where a fairly large gathering of people were present and about £680 was donated to Alder Hey, and took refreshments across the road at The Grapes pub in sight of our old farmhouse.

A part that I mentioned earlier was that there was no room in the grave for Mum as Aunty Ethel (that rock of a person who had helped Mum) had, in the meantime, been buried on top of Uncle Albert and, of course, my Dad, who probably could not believe that she had ended up on top of him! So our Mum had to go under the path at the side of the grave which meant she was nowhere near Little Bobby. For some reason, on his grave, which had his grandparents Sylvia and George Whalley, there had been a stone placed which did not have any reference to him. Later, my son Michael and I put a new stone on with both grandparents and Little Bobby's names inscribed on it (see photograph of Little Bobby).

It took a good while before I was able to feel at peace when I visited the grave of my parents. For nearly every day of forty-four years, my Mum would speak to or ring me, or make a cup of tea or a meal/snack. I hope people who read this book will perhaps see something of their own parents. If so, then this book will have been well worth my disclosing all my intimate feelings because there are still some good parents, sons and daughters. However, because of tight monitoring measures (money worries, etc), maybe they have not helped one another as much as they might, and maybe burials are a greater comfort than cremations.

Anne had become church steward by now, which is the senior position in the chapel, and I took on the position of treasurer—without doubt one of the most difficult jobs there are! So Anne helped me and I helped her. I also, together with Chris Walmsley, looked after the property which was badly in need of internal pointing (including the high ceiling). Without seeking any praise, I made a scaffold of square wooden frames ten feet tall with plywood, and braces and steps planted on top of the plywood, and together with my own height, I managed to reach twenty-odd feet. It all had to be washed and cleaned. The chapel moved into the Sunday school for four Sundays, and I was really proud to make no charge—the chapel only paying for the materials. And like when you do your own house, once you do the painting it leads on to a new carpet.

Also, the Walking Day banner was tatty so Anne and I got Anne's cousin, Robert Hawthornthwaite, to ask the leading signwriter and self-taught artist, Mr Ronnie Kitchen, to do the Ascension on one side and Samuel on the back. In total, some sixteen characters were painted, and with the help of Mary Beetham and Anne's mother, this was accomplished.

We needed funds to pay for all this. Firstly, Revd Day sat in the vestry for six hours and received gifts of money anonymously. That really was a good way of drawing money in!

Shortly after, Walmer Bridge Chapel suffered a fire through vandalism, and I did that chapel and Sunday school up as well, including a new ceiling in the chapel, and that also was a most satisfying job. But as I write this book, the chapel has sadly just closed!

Anne and I now started twenty years of fundraising. Firstly, jumble sales, which are sadly now going out of fashion, but in those days (and later) under the banner of the Much Hoole Country Fair, we were to become very well known for holding good jumbles—sometimes raising £400 (which would be £600–£700 today). I remember we were given quite a lot of good bric-a-brac, and made £1000 with good help from Peter and Margaret in an auction in about 1985. The playgroup, which operated from the Sunday school part of the chapel, were struggling for funds, as was the chapel, so we suggested we might form a committee of chapel folk and some from the playgroup, which was led by Diane Bell, Anne Prescott, Pat Ryding, and Anne Wane. On the chapel side there would be Anne Whalley, Peter and Margaret Samson, Cathryn and Phillip Howarth, Polly Sutton, Caroline Strettle and Peter Robinson. Eighteen years later there would only be Anne, Peter, Margaret, Pat Ryding, Ann Wane and myself, but we had able support from Stuart and Susan Bradley, David and Nancy Greenwood, Mary Atkinson, my good friend and accountant Harold Gaskell, Bill Kirkham, Norman Edmondson, Frank Gornall, Les Johnson, John Smith and Joe Turner.

If you can find the time to read a summary of all the shows that we put on, we were to make £70,000 profit, mostly because we had our own land. One can only think someone up there was giving us strength as all this was going on during Andrea's illness, and never once did it rain in the afternoon of the show; and yet, for the next two years after the show closed (years eighteen and nineteen) we were flooded out.

The first show we had, our main celebrity was Ricky Tomlinson, who came for £200. He showed us how to make extra money and we are still friends with him. We used to meet him when he opened new Kwiksaves!

The second show we did had Malandra Burrows from *Emmerdale* as our star. She was a really lovely girl, and her dad came with her as her minder. She also came with *Brookside* star, Jason Hope, who was a pleasant enough chap, but a little shy.

Third was Gilly Coman ('Avaline' from the TV series *Bread*). She really was just like her character in *Bread*, and she was later to crown Andrea as Sunday School Rose Queen, but has now sadly died.

Forth was Andy Crane from *Blue Peter*. He was nice enough, but considering he was a top presenter, he too came across as being quite shy.

At this time, Gilly Gorman introduced us to her agent Sal Keegan, and for those who remember the *Z Cars* police television series, you may recall her husband Bob, better known as Sergeant Blackett. She was lovely and became really good friends, and in return we too attended some of her own fundraising events in Little Hulton following the sad loss of Bob to cancer.

Fifth was Jonathan Morris ('Adrian' from *Bread*). He was the poet in the programme and he was fantastic. We thought that well of him that he was to return again to do another show for us four years later.

Derrick Evans was sixth. Perhaps the name doesn't hit you, but he was known (and still is known) as 'Mr Motivator' the keep-fit man from morning television. What a pleasure it was to be in his company. We met him on Preston train station and no one recognised him.

Seventh were Christopher Chittell (Eric Pollard from *Emmerdale*) and James Hooton (Sam Dingle, also from *Emmerdale*). They were lovely too.

Eighth was Timmy Mallett from *Wackaday*—a top Saturday morning children's programme. He was right at his peak and it was a total sell-out—there must have been some 8000 people present and it was probably our top attendance ever. He did his party piece on a stage provided by Joe Turner. It was very unfortunate that a traffic cop came along and booked some of my workers before they had moved their cars. I, Geoffrey, was not going to let him get away with that, as a few days later they got summonses, so I marched into the Lancashire Police Headquarters in Hutton (these days you can't get in through the front door, but I managed to get in), and did get to speak to an assistant chief constable, who rescinded the summonses. What makes the Police act like this? We were, after all, only just setting up.

Jonathan Morris, who at that time was starring in the *Rocky Horror Show*, made his return visit to the show. He came on the train, and in order to get him back in time for his *Rocky Horror Show* appearance in Goodwood, Janice (our daughter) went back in a small aeroplane with him. What a caring chap he was!

The tenth celebrity was Beverley Callard from *Coronation Street*

(Steve's mum). Beverley had just brought out a keep-fit video so she did a workout on the stage and, of course, did the usual signing of autographs. She even managed to get a conservatory out of a firm for free, in return for some advertising. Like us, she had a good day.

At the eleventh show, we had Michelle Collins from *EastEnders*. Both Anne and I found Michelle good to work with and she really made an effort, including coming all the way from London in a big extended limousine. It seems this firm does a lot of work for her and she made them do it at cost which was only £200. Thanks, Michelle!

Sarah Lancashire from *Coronation Street* was our twelfth guest. I have to say that we all were disappointed with her, seeing that every one of my family loved her character in *Coronation Street*. I did complain after she had at one stage spent fifteen minutes in the St John's Ambulance smoking whilst everyone waited outside. I will not say anything else.

Number thirteen was Ken Dodd and his Diddymen. We had, of course, spent years trying to get him. Sal Keegan was pulling her hair out getting him to sign a contract. I was doing live radio slots saying he was coming, but I knew he had not signed. Three days before the show, we received a phone call from the Diddymen asking for travel details, so we knew that he was coming. Sal got the contract signed two days before the show, and once again we had a full showground and couldn't find any more room for cars. The Diddymen (all four, plus a driver) arrived at 11.00 a.m. saying that they must stay in a bedroom until Ken arrived. It was also a very hot day. Ken was due at 12.30 p.m. but never arrived. Half-past one went by, then 2.00 p.m., and then 2.30 p.m. By now I was very worried. People were demanding answers as to when, if at all, he was coming. However, he finally landed just after 2.45 p.m. but my, it surely was worth it. As we entered the show ring, he would walk around before going on the stage. He had us play out loud his hit song 'Happiness', and do you know, some of us had tears in our eyes! He stopped till seven o'clock—what a day—never to be beaten!

John Savident was the fourteenth (Fred Elliott in *Coronation Street*). John was a different act to all the other celebrities, and being a large fellow himself, he was quite personal to (let's say) other larger ladies and gentlemen; and yet the children (even those well into their teens) followed him about like the Pied Piper. But he was very nice to us.

Fifteenth was Jimmy Cricket. Jimmy, as always, was a loveable chap and easy to get on with. He changed into his trademark cap and wellies and did us proud.

To all our friends we had always said that the weather could not continue treating us so well. It had been our normal practice to distribute as much profit as we could to local organisations, schools, other churches in the district, and indeed, for many years, St Michael's Church (under the guidance of Revd Harry Pugh who was a dear friend of ours). We had moved to a situation where, most years, St Michael's got the most money given to them from the show. We were, I suppose, getting tired, and there were times when we were neglecting our business.

We were trying to get a major 'star' to do the final show. However, many years ago, our friends, Bob and May Crookham, had introduced us back stage to Daniel O'Donnell. We also had another connection to him in that my cousin Kathleen and her husband Norman were also personal friends of his, and had stayed with Daniel's mother in the past. Anyway, to cut a long story short, and with thanks to the above, we met him backstage one afternoon before seeing him that night in Blackpool, and he agreed the format of the show and to appear for free if we would make a donation to one of his own charities. He would also ask John Staunton, his guitarist, to play for him so that would be two for B&B. Daniel asked if I would arrange a bed-and-breakfast nearby, and as he was appearing in Bournemouth for six days, he would travel up very late after Sunday's show so that he could appear for us on the Monday.

Daniel phoned us a couple of times over one or two things (one of which was to ask about the B&B for two), but as time got nearer we hadn't heard anything from him. I fully expected him to call us whilst he was in Bournemouth, but nothing was heard.

On the day before the show I worried all day, and decided at 7.00 p.m. that I must ring the main number at the big theatre where he was appearing (as he didn't know the address of the B&B where he was staying). I managed to get through, and I stressed to the receptionist that I was a responsible person and asked if she could get a message to Daniel. Sure enough, at 7.15 p.m., and as casual as anything, he rang and I told him about the B&B. He'd forgotten he'd asked me! He also stated that his voice was not good and he might only do one song, which was disappointing.

Come the day, the hour, we were ready! I had already built a large stage, something like Tina Turner would use (which is 'T' shaped). We now had a new minister, Revd Yvonne Pearson, who could play a trumpet, and who would do a solo piece at the show later on in the day. It was decided my Anne, together with Yvonne, would go in our car to the secret bed-and-breakfast accommodation to pick Daniel and John up, whilst I kept on top of the problems that would normally occur during the show. Sure enough, whilst they were away, the generator broke down, and Keith Bradley dashed off home to get his own generator. BBC Live Television arrived and they waited to interview Daniel live.

Daniel duly arrived and asked if he and John could be left alone in a room. The next thing that happened was that Daniel was singing, accompanied by John, and we all felt very privileged listening to him sing a hymn.

Daniel duly took to the stage and sang eight songs, gave out some jokes, and joined in David Dilworth's group of line dancers in their wellies. Fantastic! He stayed that long that the plane taking him from Manchester to Ireland had to be kept waiting. Not many people would do what he did, in that, at 11.00 p.m., he rang us from his home to thank us just as we had finished watching his interview from the show on TV and excerpts from his live show. What a way to close seventeen years of providing entertainment to the district.

A few weeks later, Anne and I went over to Ireland by ferry and stayed at John Staunton's bed-and-breakfast in Dunloe. We visited Daniel's village and went to his secretly located bungalow. It was truly remarkable to visit Phoenix Park and see the security outside the American Ambassador's residence. We met a lovely lady police officer who could not wait to get home and tell her mum that she had met someone where Daniel O'Donnell had sung in their home!

I must add that the day after we arrived (which was on Friday, just after the Twin Towers tragedy in New York) we went to The Point in Dublin to see Daniel in concert. For those that don't know, The Point is a great big converted warehouse on the docks. It was a great show, but we needed a taxi after it; and as The Point was two miles out of Dublin, we had to walk into the town centre at midnight with what seemed liked 500 more people, and we could not get a taxi to stop. Both Anne and myself were getting scared and somewhat leg weary by now. Finally, I more or less had to throw myself at the front of a taxi to get him to stop. What with pubs emptying and us moving in a crowd, some small fights were starting and it was getting desperate.

Daniel O'Donnell

*Chris Walmsley. A faithful worker for Much Hoole Methodist Chapel,
standing the attics for the country fair.*

Ken Dodd crowning the queen

Sal Keegan (wife of Bob Keegan from Z Cars)
with Derrick Evans (Mr Motivator)

Full house for Timmy Mallett

Now that I'd finished doing the Country Fairs, we decided to apply to make the land into a woodland burial ground (a dream again).

I will now write about the saga of trying to get planning permission for what eventually was to lead to us to being the first privately owned woodland burial ground in the country. I was, of course, not aware of this when we started as there are well over 200 burial grounds around the country, but they are not consecrated.

After much family discussions, we decided (without any backing from banks, etc.) that a good and locally respected architect at Bramley and Pate be asked to act on our behalf, and from that day forth Richard Bramley has taken over the project and been involved in all the triumphs and despairs that we have encountered along the way.

In 2003 Richard came down and scratched ideas that I had spent many hours dreaming about: how I could visualise it all growing into something very unique.

Having done quite a lot of building in my life, I did have experience of the way planning worked, and if you were experiencing problems it was best to step back and try another route, but not let them push you about. You must not get a rejection as it looks bad on your CV.

At this stage I must mention our deep gratitude to our next door neighbours, Elizabeth and Geoff Key, who have accepted and trusted that whatever we have proposed for this burial ground, it has been to their liking and fits in with their own ideas about the environment.

Richard Bramley advised me that with its being in the Green Belt, it is laid down in statutory form that it is an acceptable change of use from Green Belt to a burial place, i.e. a cemetery. That might be so, but in the words of the planning office, "We can't just encourage every farmer to open graveyards up". So they just sat back for twelve months and waited—I suppose behind the smokescreen of the Department of the Environment who have overall charge of the ground, i.e. water tables and soil density.

Having waited and better waited, Richard then received a request (not unexpected) for site boreholes which, having lived here for over thirty years, I knew would not be a problem. So Richard brought in an expert who would be present when these boreholes were done, and he would also do a report on water table levels and conservation matters. The tests met with approval and we hoped that would satisfy the Council. Highways, thankfully, offered no objection because we had one main rock solid item that would have stopped this development. When we bought the farm off Mr and Mrs Whittaker, they had tried to get permission to build a bungalow, but in anticipation had the foresight to get permission for a lock-up garage with access directly onto the highway; so that when we bought the farm, we readily agreed for the tenant who rented the garage to continue and he also paid the council tax.

So, of course, there we were with an opening directly onto the road which was in the perfect place next to the chapel. In other words, three–nil to us:, me being an undertaker; direct access onto the site; and, we thought, the perfect land.

Still, time was going and we didn't seem to be getting anywhere with the council. I still had to drain the land, and knew that trees had to be planted when the sap was rising, so the latest would have to be April. I could see this saga going on into next winter/spring. I felt sure that the planners were behind all this waiting, just hoping I would go away.

Out of the blue, the environment people finally made a decision in that they were again concerned about table levels and soil samples. I really felt that my dream was not going to happen. All correspondence had been to the Environment Office at Walton Summit, near Preston, through their spokesman, a Miss Turner, who I was really getting upset about as she seemed to take six weeks to answer letters. Having spoken to Richard of my concern about it now being February, and if things didn't move fast then it would be a year before the trees went in, I took it upon myself to demand that Miss Turner put me through to someone who could give a straight answer. After two calls to her, she finally relented and gave me a man's name and direct phone number— and guess what, he was based in Warrington!

I rang this man, asking him why he needed more test holes when he had some from twelve months ago. He was insistent that I do them so I asked if he could be present on Thursday (this would be Monday of the same week) so that he could view the test boreholes. His words were "Dear me, Mr Whalley, I don't leave my desk—just get them done." I couldn't believe what I was hearing! Quick as a flash I said I knew they would be perfect, and he said, if so he would withdraw his objections in his absence—and Richard viewed the test.

With not receiving any objections from the neighbours, I now knew that the planners could deal with this without going to the council committee as delegated approval, which finally did come through at the end of March. So a big rush was now on. I firstly got Mr Metcalf to drain the land again. It was well-drained already, but we needed to put the new drainpipes where we weren't planting new trees. That being done, we tried not to damage the grass which was just starting to grow. All the trees, which were over twenty feet tall and root balled, were all planted with us digging the holes by hand. Dennis and Stephen also helped, together with myself. We also kept cutting the grass so it became quite lush and manageable, finishing with the planting of the laurel hedge both sides of the new road. The new road was dug by Anne's brother, Stephen, who is also my gravedigger. What a trial of endurance we were made to go through!

Having now got the ground in good order—all drains backfilled—we now needed and wanted to have the site consecrated. I received good advice from Reverend Martyn Rogers (if I might add, a person who I have the utmost respect for) who suggested that I go and see the Diocese of Blackburn's solicitor, Mr Tom Hoyle. At the solicitors, I sat round their large boardroom table to be greeted by Tom and Robert Hall, who were both pleasantly surprised by my request to apply to them for my burial ground to become hallowed. Mr Hoyle took notes and said he would have to visit the site; I suppose to check that everything I'd told him was correct.

Tom duly visited, and his first words were "What a lovely site." He walked around the ground and said he would put things in order, which meant speaking (he thought) to the Bishop of Lancaster, but eventually it was the Revd John Goddard, Bishop of Burnley, who was to do the consecrating.

It took a few weeks to arrange and we asked some of our friends to attend the consecration. Our own Minister, Revd Kathleen Woods, unfortunately was away on church business so she asked the chairman of the North West Division of Methodism, Revd Stephen Poxon, to stand in. We were very pleased because we knew that Stephen was to become the World President of the Methodist Church. Father Brendan O'Sullivan, another good friend and local priest, took part in prayers. Revd Martyn Rogers and Revd Andrew Parkinson came to support us. The new coroner for Preston, Lancaster, Ormskirk and Chorley, Dr. Aderley, attended together with his secretary, Ms Annette Seddon, and I must mention that Annette was doing the same job when I started undertaking so it was pleasing for her to be with us that day. The Mayor of South Ribble and chairlady of the parish council also attended.

The day finally arrived with Tom's help, and a service sheet/book was printed. In church law we Methodists, and anyone not Church of England, are classed as being "dissenters". So I was to do the greeting to the Bishop at the side of the site, who was then to lead a procession—the Bishop in front with crook, then Mr Tom Hoyle and Mr Robert Hall, fully robed with wigs (see photograph), then Father B O'Sullivan, Revd S Poxon, the Mayor, Parish Council Chairlady, Richard Bramley (architect), the Whalley family, and about twenty others. They all followed on in the procession, where, in each corner, the Bishop then said a few words and drew the sign of the cross with his crook. When that was completed, we all sang "Abide With Me", together with prayers, after which we moved into the chapel next door where Anne had made refreshments. What a most moving ceremony.

Someone had informed the BBC that it had just been confirmed that we were the first consecrated woodland burial ground in the country that was privately owned. The BBC was keen to film the first funeral that would be held there. Some weeks went by before I received a request from a family to ask if we would do this particular lady's funeral at the Methodist Chapel, and she would then be buried in the woodland burial ground next door. I have no wish to reveal names, but the son-in-law's family were from a family that my mother had befriended when we were growing up, and now they were going to be involved in the first interment at our place. Having told them of the BBC's interest, they agreed to let them film part of it. The news reporter, Jill Donnally, only arrived at the last minute. She did an interview with them and I must add a very good one at that. The coffin firm of Thorley Smith were involved, and Alan Roby, a dear friend, gave an interview about biodegradable coffins. All this went on till about 4.30 p.m. and we were told that it would be on TV that night. Every time the regional news came on, we all sat around the television, but nothing appeared. We went to bed thinking what a letdown it had been, but Andrea always gets up early, and by 7.00 a.m. the following day she was shouting for us to get up as we were on the telly. We could not believe that every time the regional news came on the screen, a different part of the long interview was shown. We were screened all over the northwest, and then you could say that we were now up and running.

Jim Brown and Olive Cork

Some two years later, I was now back dreaming again! We were now conducting quite a few funerals that were for people who steadfastly left instructions that they wanted a Humanist funeral and, of course, the Church would not give them use of their building (plus there are two or three other religions that come into that category as well) so this meant that they needed a graveside funeral, which is all right in the summer but not so good in the winter. We also were in need of an outside toilet (did you know, that up to ten years ago most churches did not have a toilet?) and I am sure it's because of blood pressure pills that everyone seems to want to go on so often!

I instructed the architect, Richard Bramley, to do a drawing to send to South Ribble Borough Council outlining our proposals. We thought that the new planning officer, Jill Swainson, was lukewarm towards the proposal, but she decided that it must be pushed back. We then set a site meeting up and she asked if we would withdraw the proposal. I think that was because of a time limit that government put on these things re decisions. We also needed fresh letters of support. Revd Kathleen Wood sent a good letter as did our neighbours. I also got Tom Hoyle to write an official one in which he mentioned that support would come from the diocese as well. I took the new plans to Jill Swainson who shocked me by saying she was leaving. That meant we more or less had to start again!

It is pleasing to know that the neighbours did not complain, but it was to be another six months before we were able to make progress, and eighteen months since it was first mentioned. The building had to be moved back and further back, and then lowered, but as I write this book I am about to start on the biggest venture of my life, which will not only give me a chapel, but also an office to conduct arrangements for the burial ground and bring my office work under the same roof.

SHIRE HORSES

As periodically mentioned in this book, my love is shire horses. Maybe it's in the genes going back to Lord Edgerton at Tatton Hall through my paternal grandparents (and probably generations before as we are steeped in farming history—as is my wife's side of the family).

I see these new starters coming into the showing world with their pockets full of money and who pump food into their horses. Anyone can get a horse or foal fat, but the secret is to keep them just right for what they were bred for—which, of course, is work.

"Blossom" in Walking Day pictured with Jim Coulton, Geoff's brother Edwin and brother-in-law Stephen

I have always had at least one horse that could work and was very quiet. At one time, I was doing about ten church walking days a year, with a brass band playing at the front of us or directly behind in a procession. This relied on my horsemanship and training as, previously, horses were used to working every day in towns or on the land.

Having been fortunate in being able to buy Goose Green Farm (and more land at a later time), I bought my first shire from Mr Jackson at Bartle (which is near Preston), it being a mare called Charnock Queen, who was in foal to a well known stallion, Stanley House Prince. Bad luck struck again! The evening she was getting ready to foal, our daughter Janice broke her arm so Anne and I spent most of the night at the hospital. When we eventually got back home, the mare had just foaled—a filly with three white legs. The foal can take an hour sometimes to get up and many times, just with the mare licking it, it seems to stimulate itself, and then it will get to the teat and draw the colostrum milk which is very important. Anyway, it was a nice foal, but it did seem weak, and I decided to leave it for four hours, fully expecting it to do all right, but at 5.00 a.m. I was making no progress. (Unless you have tried it yourself, you will appreciate it's not easy to lift a foal up, keep it up, and get it to bend its head to find the teat.) I now decided it was time to send for Mr Hey, the well-known horse vet, but as he arrived, the foal died. Looking back, there must have been something badly wrong as it should have lived longer, even without milk.

To move on, we put the mare in foal using Jimmy Walker's horse, and it came twelve months later with a colt foal which did well. About ten months later, the mare, being about sixteen years old, suddenly went off her food. Mr Hey was at a loss, and we were forced to put her down. She went to the knacker's yard for a post mortem, where we found out that it was liver trouble (which can be caught from the urine of rats), and inside her was a colt foal which, of course, was also dead.

Having been used to setbacks, I knew of a black gelding for sale that had been worked and I bought it off Mr John Suckley of Oswestry. It was a decent horse but never as quiet as it should have been, and one day it kicked the yearling colt and broke its jaw. For some strange reason, we took it to the veterinary hospital but they couldn't do anything and that horse was put down as well. Three losses in three years!

Daffodil at Croston Coffee Day, at two years old, her first day out in a procession with Norman helping out

I bought another gelding from Bob Gardner, which was part of the Hull Brewery turnout. I found out later that this horse was the lazy one of the pair, but I put up with him for three years. I then took him to Beeston Horse Sales and got the top price of the day! So I carried on to John Suckley's and bought an old grey mare which was the making of me.

This old grey mare was nearly white and a good worker. The day after we'd got her, me and Old Jim Coulton put her in the tip cart and we both fell in love with her. She was sixteen years old, and Anne's dad said you should never bother with old horses and old women! (Anne's mother used to tell him off for that!)

Norman, Geoff and Brian at Preston Guild which happens once every 20 years

The mare's pedigree name was Stuntney Complacent and we decided to give her the name Blossom, and she was super! She did a lot of processions—liked the band being near her—and she bred a few foals. Eight years later she died.

I had now traced Blossom's pedigree back and found that it went back to 1864, and she'd come from the Stuntney Hall Farm Estate in Ely, Cambridgeshire. (In all that time, these horses have only either been on our farm, or the one at Stuntney.)

At that time, I decided I would like to take my holidays in that area as the Stuntney Estate was still going strong and they still had fourteen shires. I was later to find out that they had registered over three percent of all shires, more than anyone else in the world! In their prime they would have ninety foals each year, which is a tremendous amount.

An interesting thing happened whilst we were on holiday visiting Ely Cathedral. We got talking to one of the vergers who wanted to know where we came from. I told him of our interest in the shires of Stuntney Estate. His eyes lit up, and he said he would get someone to meet up with us, and he brought a lovely lady of about sixty-five to see us.

The lady was Miss Beryl Lee, who sat down with us while we had some refreshments. She told us her life story in which she was forced to give up her job and look after her aged parents. As a sort of pleasurable pastime, she would walk about four miles every day, all weathers, to see the horses at the Stuntney Estate to give them a pet, and a carrot, of course. She knew old Blossom, but Blossom was known to her as Jolly. She told how one of the workers let her know that Jolly was leaving the next day, so all she could think about was that she must go and say her sad farewells. With tears rolling down her face, she never for one moment thought she would ever hear anything more about Jolly, knowing that she was going to a dealer in Wales.

It was the beginning of a very true friendship where every month we were to receive the most beautiful handwritten letters (about five pages long—both sides) keeping us informed about what was happening on the farm, at Ely Cathedral, and in her own life too. We were invited back to her own little quaint terrace house with no mod cons, and we would regularly take her out for rides in the car around the surrounding villages and towns. In everything she did, she was a very religious person. It was very sad that that part of our lives came to an end. Some people reading this book may not understand the deep effect this little woman had on our lives, especially with little Andrea being so ill. God bless you, Beryl Lee!

MY BELOVED SHIRE HORSES

In 1949 my father sold his last workhorse and bought a John Brown tractor off Barton Motors in Preston, probably because of his good friend, Clarence Ellison. The John Brown was blessed with a double seat, which meant Mother could travel with Dad and, when at the field, Mother could steer it in a straight line (or just about) whilst Dad loaded the trailer or whatever, but these new fangled things did flood a lot and there were times when, if only we had had a work horse, at least the workman would have been able to go to the fields, as most of our land was some distance away.

So Dad knew of a grey workhorse that Dick Cropper, a horse dealer from Banks, had acquired, so off we went—Dad, my younger brother and I liked what we saw. Dad liked the horse, and us two kids were encouraged to walk under its belly. It did prove to be a good sort of horse. It stood for ages at the gate in the entrance to a stockyard, and I used to try and be brave and climb up the gate and hold the head collar, and try and slip my leg over its back. Just as I was putting all my weight on its back, it just slid away. I don't know what would have happened if it had remained still and I was sat on it like a cowboy.

Those people old enough will recall names of the Shire Horse Studs in Lancashire—the Badshaws, Ainscoughs, Shaws, and the Suttons, who were one of the biggest Studs in England and at one time would have over fifty stallions. One of their best stallions was The Bomber, one of the best in England at that time, but because of the war many of their horses were put down for meat or castrated for work by order of the War Department, all within ten miles of where I have always lived.

In 1953, with Dad having died, Mother had to get out of the farm (which was a tenant farm) so she had to have a farm sale to get rid of

the implements and animals. The sale was not very big so some of
the local farmers put their unwanted harness and bits-and-bobs in, the
money to go to Mum. Some of the farmers were Forshaws, Bakers,
Dandys—still good friends some sixty years later.

Apart from Uncle George and Aunty Kitty taking us to the Royal
Lancashire Show, I took a back seat from farming, apart from looking
after Mum's hens. God, how I hated cleaning hen cabins out. I can itch
now just thinking about it.

Now married and living in a semi-detached house, a small holding
came up for sale in 1975. I was able, with a struggle, to purchase it
with two acres, and was able to add more land later, and then was up
and running. I gained some experience with a couple of light horses.
My wife's father told me that Ernie Jackson had a shire filly and a shire
mare for sale. He bought one and I the other—called Charnock Queen,
a real shire, twelve years old, in foal. On the evening she was due to
foal, our eldest daughter Janice broke her arm playing, so her Mum
and I took her to hospital and got home about 9 p.m. The mare had
just foaled a filly by Stanley House Black Prince, owned by the great
horseman Robert Hull, whose funeral, incidentally, I was to conduct
many years later. He left instructions that half a bale of straw must be
placed in the grave before his coffin.

To return to the foal, we could not get the filly to suck. You do get
them now and then where they go to the wrong end every time, and
it died later. These days, with tubing pouring the first milk into its
stomach, it perhaps would not have happened.

I next became involved with Jimmy Walker ('Weston' prefix) of
Westhoughton. I had a good relationship with Jimmy, who had at that
time a magnificent dapple grey stallion, Aneland Masterpiece. He
would make these present-day stallions look like half-legged ones! I
believe he had the habit of walking across the yard to meet his mare
on his hind legs. That is some sight to witness, but there is a way of
controlling that and Jimmy did it to him and put him on his backside,
but you run the risk of giving him an injury—not something a novice
should do, and that will hopefully stop that bad habit.

I was now wanting to put a horse in a walking day so I needed a good quiet horse and harness. I was at John Harvey's reduction sale and got talking to a man who had in his possession a set of show harness which I bought; but still needed that good quiet horse. I bought a black gelding off John Suckley from Oswestry, but it was not quite enough for the job I needed so I then bought a bay gelding from Bob Gardner which had been in a pair at Hull Brewery. It would seem that it let the other one do all the work, but Bob knew I was not pleased. There was a shire sale coming up at Beeston Auctions and I put the gelding in the sale. He was a good-looking type and I got my money back, and carried on to John Suckley's where I knew he had just got an old mare which had been served by Elaine Grey King. She, of course, was Stuntney Complacement, whom we met a few pages ago.

My old friend, Jim Coulton, came to visit us when she arrived, put some harness on, put her in a box cart and off we went. Old Jim was in raptures about how she could use the collar left or right, back and go forward when commanded. She was just perfect. I was to find out later that Decker Murfitt and his sons had broken her in. Everybody in the Fens knows how good they are with horses. My ill daughter would stand for hours in her cot looking at Blossom, and Blossom would spend hours looking back. We always said we owed a lot to that horse for keeping Andrea's spirits up. She did many walking days and loved the band—nothing scared her. She had four more foals up to twenty-one years of age and then seemed to stiffen up and start showing her age, and at twenty-three years she was put down and buried at Goose Green Farm. Thou good and faithful servant.

Dakka had kept in touch and told us that Blossom's daughter, Stuntney Irene, known as Diamond, could be bought, and had been broken at two years old but not worked for nine years. On his recommendation I bought her, and after a few months she started to prove as good as her mother.

What also was pleasing was that she was in foal to Ruskington King (King William). The foal finally came, and it was a colt—a good one—which was later sold to a Jack Fordon, from Manchester

94

way. Well, what is interesting is that Jack died not long after, and Ray Williams started his illustrious career by buying that colt; and, of course, everybody knows that Ray went to the very top in shires and his Moorfield prefix is known the world over.

Richard Thomas: two-year-old stallion about to be rejected. What rubbish!

Now sixteen years old, Blossom left a colt foal by Park Head Super Star, which was dark brown and which we called Goose Green's Richard Thomas; and at two years old (see photo) he was about to go in front of the inspection panel and vet. Mr Worthington and Mr Hiles rejected him because they alleged that he had a couple of blemishes under his heels, which could turn to grease later. What rubbish! I took him home, rang my shire vet (Tom Hey) and asked him to call that day. I told him I would pay him whatever he asked for, and he came within a couple of hours and could not find anything wrong. That very same day I lodged an appeal, was made to send £100—a lot of money in those days—to the Shire Society. Two weeks later, Mr Yates and Mr Williamson came to our farm. They informed me that they were not aware of the reason for turning him down; and guess what, all they could find was one hock slightly puffed and that was only because the horse had been kept in waiting for them. My wife made their lunch, and whilst eating, Jim offered to buy him. I said no, took him back next year to the National Show, and he was fifth. I was only turned down, in my opinion, to stop a younger man having a stallion. Unfortunately, three years later, on a very cold New Year's afternoon, he had gone through the ice in a pit where he drank from. Together with the Fire Brigade, we got him out and got him home. He died the day after. Why didn't I take Jim's offer?

Diamond went on and did very loyal service, and whilst we used champion stallions, she never seemed to breed anything as good as herself. However, when she was eighteen years old a filly was born. It was a very plain sort with two black forelegs and dark brown. I never got any offers for her so I ended up keeping her. Usually as yearlings they can be silly, but this filly, whom we had by then given the name Goose Green Daffodil, was developing into a lovely sweet-natured lanky filly, so I started to break her in for work. I then sent her to Bob Hull to be put in foal and to see if he would do some road work with her. Anne and I went past Bob's farm one night and saw all these visiting mares all stood around a gate—but no Daffodil. When I looked in a far corner, there she was. It was so pitiful—which made me get her home the next day. She was so lonely; she was probably being bullied, with being so young.

Diamond died when twenty-one years and is buried here at Goose Green Farm (see photo of Daffodil at Croston Coffin Day as a two-year-old with Andrea, and a good friend of mine, Norman Edmondson).

At five to six months gone, Daffodil aborted her foal—something she was to do eight times over fourteen years. I said to Steven, my helper, that we must get our own stallion as I could not keep spending this sort of money. My good friend in Devon, Basil Pike, who I have done quite a few deals with, told me of an old stallion, not very big, but of good

At the National Shire Horse Show, Peterborough one of the most colourful and respected Shire horse members, Basil Pike from Devon, received the Sir Anthony Crossman Medal for his devoted service to the Shire horse (see also page 41).

Basil was born into a farming family and moved to Middleton Barton in 1937, from where he still farms. His father was asked to visit his dying landlord who wished him to buy the farm. Basil recounts how his father needed to be persuaded to buy; money being tight. The landlord advised him to cut down some trees and he would soon recoup enough to pay for the farm, which he did.

Eventually Basil took over, married Frances and had two children. Jean grew up and married a farmer, but sadly her husband died. Basil's son, Frank and his wife Mary, now work with him and run a large dairy herd. Sadly Frances has also died.

Basil and Frank have a good partnership in that Basil is able to utilise the grazing and breed, buy and sell Shire horses. Indeed, it is said that nearly every horse enthusiast in Devon and Cornwall, as well as the surrounding counties, will have had dealings with Basil at some time or other. He has also sold many Shire horses overseas, mostly to Holland.

Basil has always bred and bought store cattle and is well-known for the quality of his bulls, usually hiring them out. Today, you still see him at most auctions, always doing a deal.

Among his other interests are his presidency of his local skittle league for 40 years, his long-standing membership of the Countryside Cavalcade, and his involvement with local ploughing associations. He was chief Shire steward at Honiton Show, a panel judge for the Shire breed and a keen supporter of all

Surprise evening for South West's man of Shires

local outdoor events including local stag and fox hunts.

In February many of his friends met at the Merry Harrier, Westcott, Cullompton – a total surprise to him – for a meal and a nostalgic evening organised by Geoff and Anne Whalley, with help from Jenny Tuckett and Molly and Jim Bennett. Many friends travelled long distances to attend, including Brian Cooper from Basingstoke and Nick Rayner and Dorothy Mouland from the New Forest.

The Shire Horse Society's chief executive, Andrew Mercer, travelled from Peterborough to give a moving speech describing the sterling work Basil has done to keep the Shire and shows going in the South West of England, and the love and respect shown to Basil from many walks of life.

An auction for the Tsunami Appeal was conducted by David Jeffreys and a memorable evening was concluded by local auctioneer, Stafford Sampson: a very jovial speech for a good man!

Top, Basil Pike driving his Shire to a flat lorry loaded with bags of coal during a promotion for the Shire Horse Society's report History with a Future *in Honiton in the late 1980s. Centre, Basil Pike received his 30-year medal from Shire Horse Society president Mr Walter Gilbey at this year's Shire Horse Show. Left, surprise, surprise! Gathering of the clan in February to celebrate Basil's contribution to the Shire breed.*

Tribute to Basil Pike

temperament, who stayed out all winter and ran out with mares and foals. Mrs James had him and I agreed to hire him with the possibility of buying him later. When we arrived to collect him, he didn't look very big although he had travelled to meet up with us. I looked him up in the Stud Book and I was amazed to see that, although he had a Welsh name, he was in effect Diamond's daughter's son: Penygarn Wheelers Gift, and that his mother was Stuntney Jean. I spoke with his Welsh owner and was told no way would he sell as Jean was such a dear to them. Mr Pike said the travellers had also used him for a while. I then was in a situation where he was a half-brother to Daffodil, but after taking advice from experts, used him on Daffodil. Guess what—Daffodil held, with help from pig's histamine given every day. We got a living filly next year, a colt called Daniel O'Donnell; missed the following year; and then got a bay filly which later turned dapple grey and was now called Goose Green's Olive's Joy. The filly has grown up into one of the best brood mares in the country. We never called the stallion any special name, but his reputation went before him and nearly every mare he served he left in foal. When about twenty-two years of age, with hardly any teeth, he was put down and buried in what we call the "Stallion Field".

As I mentioned before, I had come across the great shire vet Tom Hey, of Rufford, Ormskirk. Many times he was to call and attend my animals. He seemed to sleep for only three hours a day, but spent much of the night visiting sick animals. If you needed a vet you had to stay up well into the night to greet him. We always invited him to judge the pets at Much Hoole Country Fair that we ran for many years, and how he looked forward to it—a real James Herriott—and not forgetting his dear wife Elsie, who always accompanied him.

Tom arranged his own funeral and he requested that our very good workhorse called Daffodil take him on a flat lorry to church, and that burial people lined the route—a great honour for me. Anne, myself, and all his clients were invited to a banquet at The Mill, Croston where Ginger McCain (former trainer of the legendary racing horse Red Rum, then from Southport) gave a speech. I think Tom looked after Red Rum.

I must here mention Tom's veterinary practice. He was in partnership with John Greenwood, who was a cattle and pig man. Another much-respected vet, Seamus Miller, has now taken Tom's role on, and together with Clare Sutcliffe and Shona, look after all our horses and are thought highly of by us all.

John Wesley: Winner of the best grey colt at National Show

Snelson Naomi; I bought this yearling off John Williams of Snelson, Cheshire, and broke her in. I have to say she took to work well, and was another dream filly who went on to have mostly colts—one called Goose Green's Sunny Jim after a good friend of ours, Jim Brown. Another colt we called Goose Green's John Wesley. A flower festival was being held next door at our Methodist chapel on the day he was born so it was fairly obvious we would call him John Wesley, who went on to win best grey colt at the National Show—what a proud day for me. The National was held on the day that a hurricane was blowing over the Midlands and it got him upset. Marquees, etc., were blowing away, and as the president held the cup, John Wesley upped with his front knees and knocked the cup up in the air, and landed on his bottom. I just said to him, "Get up you daft beggar", which he did, and I took him back into his box; and the first thing he did as I was taking his tail out was that he kicked out with two feet, and so he was soon on his way. I wasn't having that.

Anne and I have had a good friendship with Jenny Tucket, who lives in Ide, in Exeter, from whom I have bought her unwanted colts and fillies over the years, one of which is Goose Green's Charles Wesley (not John Wesley!), who is the sire of Goose Green's Perfection, national champion two-year-old gelding 2013, whose dam is Goose Green's Olive's Joy—and her dam, Goose Green's Daffodil. What a feeling it was to take a national championship after forty years of trying, with our own breeding from, you might say, good quiet work horses.

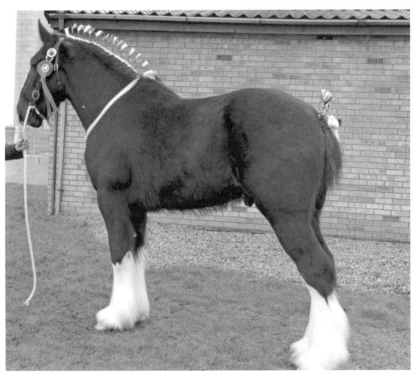

Goose Green's Perfection, two-year-old gelding, champion at National Show, 2013

Another colt by Decoy Georgie was Goose Green's Saint George. Kings bought it off me a few weeks before the 2010 National Show, which won three-year-old gelding champion, junior champion and senior champion.

Goose Green's Saint George, National Champion Gelding 2010

As well as winning in the national show mentioned above, he also went on to win:

The Arthur Rule Memorial Award to the Junior Champion Gelding. Breeder: G C Whalley

The Mrs Stanton Perpetual Silver Challenge Cup for Champion Gelding: Breeder G C Whalley

The Society's Silver Spoon to the Champion Gelding. Breeder: G C Whalley

Champion Gelding Prize from Robert (Bob) Jones. Breeder: G C Whalley

The late Miss Jane Smith Special Award. Breeder: G C Whalley.

What a feeling of pride. (Goose Green's Marshall Y Knott was sire of ridden horse National Champion.)

Goose Green's Grey Ambassador—National Champion Grey Colt

Itersey Grey Princess: one I broke in, and is currently doing the wedding circuit in Barnsley, and much loved by Karen who has three more of our horses there as well. And as I go through the proofs of this week, I have had two colt foals born, a grey and a black, all breeding going back to 1860. The grey one Joseph, the black one Tom Finney.

Joseph and Tom Finney together with their mums

When going to Devon to buy foals, we have been privileged to be made most welcome by Basil Pike and family, Jenny and John, and I must not forget Molly and Jim Bennett. It has always been a delight to have a meal out with them and I once had the chance to visit Denys Benson of East Hanningfield Hall—what a delightful man, who made us very welcome and who did much to keep the shires going when at their lowest numbers. What was always interesting was that he also had a graveyard at the back of where he lived which would have been a vicarage once. We were told that relatives of people already there would often bring ashes—how lovely.

Some years ago I introduced Tony Gibson's Shire Secretary and Field Officer John Ward, to Royal Liver Assurance, Liverpool, with hope of getting the National Show sponsored, and that day in Liverpool really opened my eyes to what was happening behind the scenes. I could never go public about what I was told, but I just hope that people never lose the will to use fair play and remember that shires played such a big part in our history, and that with this mixing of blood will take the character and weight of the horse away.

I spent half a day with Mr Stockdale, Isle of Ely. What a privilege to have met him in person and listened to his reminiscing about their family working and showing shire horses, and his knowledge of Cole Ambrose Limited. I am very fortunate to have the complete set of Stud Books in mint condition, most of them belonging once to the top breeder, G. R. C. Foster, owner of the greatest grey mare that ever walked this earth: Erfyl Lady Grey. See the picture in Keith Chivers' book *The Shire Horse*. They could be bought if the person would keep them all intact.

Penygarn Wheeler's Gift stallion when he was 24

Daffodil with an orphan foal

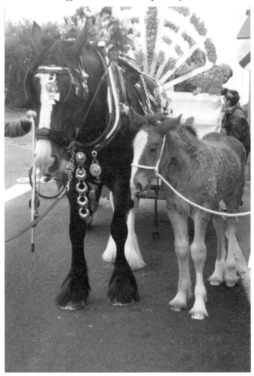

Daffodil with Olive's Joy. A job well done

Whilst I am remembering all my horses, past and present, I must mention Brian Taylor and his family who live not far from me, who I see most days walking his dog out. This family have suffered much in life. The first Mrs Taylor died young from an awful illness leaving young children who Brian has done a sterling job in bringing up. I knew his daughter, Laura, loved horses, visited my own horses, and that she was working for a racing stable in Ireland. But in the winter of 2013, I was asked by Brian to conduct a funeral for Laura who had sadly died. There would be a funeral where she lived, organised by her boss (none other than Aidan O'Brien, the famous Irish racehorse trainer) and we would bring her home to Much Hoole for a cremation.

I write this as a remembrance to a good young woman who, in her special job, rose to become one of Aidan's top riders and grooms, and when you think of all the top stallions and mares, she would have handled… unbelievable! Good on you, Laura.

Brian and his wife have shown great strength in coming through all this. Well done to Brian and his family, and yet another achiever from this tiny village of Much Hoole.

Finally, I must acknowledge those that, in my opinion, brought the shire horse back from its darkest hour, and for that reason alone the more times they are written about, the more we shall remember them:

Roy Bird

David Kay

Captain Courage

The Ward family

Jim Yates

Jim Walker

Bob Hull

D. Denson

Basil Pike

Geoff Morton

John Suckley

Keith Chivers and Edward Hart, who both wrote great books about shires.

Terry Keegan, who gave many hours on committees to keep the harness section going.

Christopher Zeuner OBE and his good lady. Diana Zeuner, who have filled a big space in the shire history with keeping the *Shire Horse Magazine* in existence, especially its quality. It was sad that Chris died, but Diane has done really well in keeping it going, and it's made old men happy on a winter's night to glance through these magazines which come out four times a year. I know, like me, they will enjoy looking at past editions, too.

Tony Gibson, the show secretary, asked if our daughter Andrea would, on behalf of the Shire Horse Society, present a bouquet of flowers to Her Royal Highness The Princess Royal at St James's Palace when she invited the society to a fundraising evening when she was president, for which we were very proud.

SHIRE HORSE SOCIETY

The Deputy Presidents cordially invite

MISS. A. H. WHALLEY

to a Reception in

St James's Palace

in the presence of

HRH The Princess Royal

TUESDAY MARCH 14TH 2000
6.30PM - 8.30PM

Dress: Lounge Suits

Invitation to St James' Palace for Andrea to present flowers on behalf of the Shire Horse Society

Andrea presenting flowers to Her Royal Highness The Princess Royal

And that is a brief history of my dealings up to now with the shire horses and the prefix "Goose Green". I think my Grandad Royle would have been very proud. At the moment, I have ten shires of all ages, and I will always have one or two for sale.

One last point to mention, which might be of interest to farmers. Whilst looking into our family history, we found newspaper cuttings from old *Liverpool Mercury* and *Warrington Guardian* newspapers, which we believe relate to my great-great-great-grandfather, Joseph Stringer, dated 9th April 1859, and which stated:

"Freak of Nature. On Sunday morning last, a cow was delivered of a double calf, having two perfect heads, eight legs, and two tails, and otherwise a complete double calf. The cow was the proprietor of Mr James Smith, Penny Peck Farm, Cowley, near Arley. The calf had to be cut away from the cow under the superintendence of Mr Joseph Stringer, farmer, Crowley."

An amazing story!

My mother's sister, Aunty Barbara, was asked by my sister Monica some years ago if she would write down the history of my mother's side, the Wagstaffs, leading to wherever they came from, but with modern technology and help from a direct relative from the Florence/Wagstaff side of the family, we have been shocked at what has arisen. We had felt sure that all the four family lines would have been farmers/farm labourers. My mother's nephew, John, a retired policeman, has been in touch with me, and all he knew was that his father said, "Don't even think about going down that road—leave well alone" when asked if he knew anything about the family history—and he has been as shocked as any of us. What we found is probably why my mother kept quiet about her side of the family, apart from her mum being such a good person. The Wagstaffs and the Florences had joined up together by both brothers and sisters marrying into both sides, and thus creating a criminal element—the Florences being travellers/hawkers/poachers, with both sides trying to keep one step ahead of the law, especially in regard to a prolific railway robbery. (I have enclosed newspaper transcripts of quite a few court cases, and I just thought they were interesting for people to read. We have not edited them. These can be found at the end of this chapter.)

All I have known about my grandmother, Frances Wagstaff, is that Little Bobby, my brother, was taken ill at her farm for which, following his death, my father laid the blame on my grandmother, accusing her of neglect—which opinion, of course, my mother was later to tell me that she did not share, but that would be the way Dad's mind would work. All I was ever told from mother was that she was a lovely person.

In 2012, whilst my daughter was tracing our family tree, a member of the Wagstaff family got in touch to tell her that she could surf the net and find court cases in the *Stafford Journal* regarding my grandmother's father, George Wagstaff. George Wagstaff married a Sarah Jane Florence whose brother, John, was involved in quite a few run-ins with the law; and John Florence married George Wagstaff's sister. John Florence was a bad lad, was arrested many times, for poaching and other crimes, and was sent to prison on numerous occasions with "hard labour". One such charge involved him being arrested for dangerous driving whilst driving his pony and trap through town, and the policeman stated that "he caused people to fly", but later his own child was run over by a pony and trap outside his house. Both George Wagstaff and John Florence committed what appeared to be the crime of the year when they stole a rail wagon full of silk ties, calico, etc., and were both sent to prison, with others, and again got "hard labour" (see attached court case documents). On the census for the Florence/Wagstaff families it gives their occupations as hawkers, spectacle-makers, horse dealers; and they would be travelling round the Staffordshire area selling wares from the back of their horse and cart. They even gave their children traditional traveller names, such as Sabrina.

For three days after being given this information, I was in great shock. I have had many run-ins with travellers (and not many months ago I had my registration plates taken from one of our estate vehicles, plus some lead also), although someone told me that this is probably where I get my keen interest in shire horses from. But to this day, I cannot understand why my mother never mentioned such an important matter affecting us all, especially with all the newspaper evidence. As I have mentioned earlier in this book, Frances Wagstaff is buried on her own in Croston Cemetery and she won't be forgotten!

I Went Down That Road

Burton Weekley News – Friday May 10, 1867

Shocking Accident – On Friday afternoon last, about 4 o'clock, a child named Alice Florence was accidentally killed in Horninglow-street, Burton. From what we gather it appears that the poor child, who was ony two years of age, left its mother while she was at work in the house and ran out of the door into the street. The mother followed, but only in time to see her child underneath the legs of a horse drawing one of the commissioner's carts which was passing at the time, and before the animal could be stopped the wheels had passed over the unfortunate infant, killing it on the spot. Not the slightest blame is attributed to the driver of the cart, who did all in his power to prevent the lamentable occurrence.

Burton Weekley News and General Advertiser – Thursday 12th November 1874

Shooting without a Licence – John Florence was charged with having used a gun for the purpose of killing game on the 6th inst., without having taken out the necessary licence – Raymond Lathbury said he resided at Wetmore. On the morning of the 6th inst, about 7.30, he was in a field, and saw the defendant shoot over a fence at a covey of birds. He followed him, and lost sight of him when near the bridge, which runs off the Derby-road. He turned back again, and met the defendant in a lane face to face, and asked what his name was. Defendant gave it as John Stokes, New-street. After walking about for some time, he started for Horninglow, and he accompanied him, and took him to P.E. Steele's house, where he gave his name as John Florence. Defendant in reply to the charge said "I shot at the bird, but did not hit it, more's the pity." He afterwards returned to the place where he met defendant, and found a partridge on the bridge, still warm. He saw defendant pick the bird up – Fined 40 and costs.

Burton Weekley News and General Advertiser – Thursday 8th August 1878

Assaults – John Florence was charged with having on the 3rd inst., assaulted William Crump. – The defendant met him in Horninglow-Street, on the above date, carrying a jug. He knocked the jug out of his hand, and he told the defendant he would have to pay for it. Defendant then gave him a severe beating. He went in quest of a policeman, after he escaped from the defendant and during the time he was away, the defendant, who lives at the back of prosecutors house, brought a gun out of the house and threatened to shoot the first man who laid hands on him. – Fined 20s, and 12s 6d cost.

Burton Weekley News and General Advertiser – Thursday 22nd August 1878

Tuesday, August 20th (Before Sir Tonman Mosley, Bart., J H Griffiths and H Wardle Esq)

Extensive Robbery from The North Stafford Railway

John Florence, labourer, of Bee-Hive Yard, and Joseph Page, labourer of Stretton, were charged with having on the 24th June last, stolen three gross of silk ties, and four gentlemen's leather bags, the property of the North Stafford Railway - Case remanded for a week to complete the evidence.

John Florence, Joseph Page (two defendants in the previous case), George Wagstaff, labourer, of Little Burton, and Herbert Bull, were charged with having, on the 10th July last, stolen one truss, the property of the North Stafford Railway Co, containing 100 yards of white calico, 98¼ yards of flannel, 33¾ yards of plain calico sheeting, 22 pairs of stockings, 36 yards of linen flax, 25 yards of dress lawns, and other articles value £12 9s 0d.

Mr Payne, of Hanley, prosecuted, and Mr Wilson, defended.

Thomas Adams said he was a draper's assistant in the employ of Messrs. Dunicliff of Uttoxeter. On the 10th July last, he assisted to pack a truss of goods for the branch establishment at Burton. The articles produced were a portion of the goods which he packed. He saw two trusses, and one skip delivered to the Railway Company on the 10th of July.

John William Clewley, draper's apprentice, gave similar evidence.

Augustus Hall said he was a carter in the employ of the North Stafford Railway Company, at Uttoxeter. On the 10th July last, he received two trusses and one skip from Messrs. Duncliff to be sent to their branch establishment at Burton. He delivered them to the shipping clerk, together with the consignment note.

Thomas Turner, shipping clerk in the employ of the Company, proved receiving the goods which be entered on an invoice.

James Keeling, foreman porter, in the employ of the company at Uttoxeter, proved receiving two trusses, and a skip from Messrs. Dunicliff, of Burton. They were placed in wagon No. 1792. The Wagon was labelled to go from Uttoxeter, to Horninglow-Street, Burton. The Wagon was covered with a sheet, securely tied down.

George Holder said he was a checker at the Horninglow-street Station, Burton. At 7.45 am, on the 11th July, he entered in the book produced the goods taken from the wagon 1792. There was only one truss and one skip, for Dunicliff and Son. He took his book in the office to have it checked with the invoice.

Frederick Archer said he was a checker, at the Horninglow-street Station. On the morning of the 11th of July last, the above witness brought a book to him. On checking his book with invoice, he found there was a truss missing, and he wrote across the invoice "only one truss received here".

John Compton Dunicliff said he was in business at Burton, as a draper, in conjunction with his father. On the 11th of July last, he received an invoice from his establishment at Uttoxeter, and he had not received the whole of the goods mentioned in it. He had only received one truss and one skip. He told the carter there was a truss missing, and subsequently he sent in a claim to the company for £17 13s 2d the value of the missing truss. He gave a list of the missing articles, to the detective of the Railway Company.

P.e. Spendlove said on Sunday last he was on duty in Princess-

Street, Burton, in company with P.e. Drumm, in plain clothes. Between nine and ten in the morning they met the defendant Bull, who was carrying something bulky in his pocket. They stopped him, and asked him what he had got in his pocket, and he replied that it was a pocket-handkerchief. They let him go, and afterwards followed him into Waterloo-Street, and they searched him. He found on him a dress-piece, and P.e. Drumm found another piece. He found a pair of stockings in an inside pocket, and he was wearing a similar pair. On asking him where he obtained them he replied "under a hedge at Anslow". They brought him to the police-station, and locked him up. Knowing his associates he went to Wagstaff's house, and searched the premises. He found a quantity of sheeting in a corner of the room, a smock, two toilet covers, flannel, braid, flax, white calico, and a quantity of articles. He arrested Wagstaff and on charging him with the offence he said "I did not steel them, they were brought to me house by Florence, and I took them in out of kindness, for I married his sister."

Sergeant Buckley said he in company with Mr. Superintendent Bowen went to Page's house. On searching it he found a quantity of flannel, sheeting, and other articles which were identified as stolen property. In a shed at the back of his house, he found a pair of shoes which were also identified by Mr. Dunicliff, as his property. He arrested Page, and on charging him he did not make any reply.

P.e. Buggy went to Bull's House on Sunday evening, and found one pair of stockings with Dunicliff's private mark on concealed in a pillow slip. He also found several other articles.

Mr Superintendent Bowe, proved searching Florence's house, and found several collars, toilet covers, a quantity of calico, and other articles, which were all identified. He arrested Florence who made no reply to the charge.

All the defendants were committed for trial at Stafford Quarter Sessions, bail being refused.

Burton Weekley News and General Advertiser – Thursday, August 29, 1878

"The Railway Robberies"

At the police-court of Tuesday, before Sir Tonman Moseley, Bart., Joseph Page, John Florence and Herbert Bull were again brought up on a charge of stealing three leather travelling bags and a gross of silk ties, value £6 6s, on the 24th June, the property of the North Staffordshire Railway Company. Mr Paine, of Hanley, appeared to prosecute, and Mr Wilson defended. The neckties were consigned by Mr Coates, manufacturer, of London, to Mr S Herratt junr, of High-street, on June 22nd, and were duly despatched to Burton in wagon No. 7887 from King's Cross Station. The wagon reached Tutbury, and on June 24th Thomas Harrison, foreman porter at Tutbury Station, checked the goods contained therein with the invoice, and found them all right. He afterwards placed the parcel in question in wagon No. 2485, and that was despatched to Horninglow-street Station, after having been again checked by John Stanbrook, number taker. The wagon arrived at the Horninglow-street Station on the 25th June, and George Holden, a checker, checked the goods contained in it, but did not find any parcel addressed to Mr. Herratt. He took his box to the office, where the contents of the wagon, as reported by him, were checked with the invoice by Frederick Archer, check clerk. He found that the parcel for Mr. Herratt had not arrived, and a notice to that effect was made on the invoice. As the ties did not reach Mr Herratt he sent in a claim for £4 13s. In June, Messrs Herratt and Son, also of High Street, gave an order to Messrs Lyon and Son, of London, for three bags, which were duly forwarded, but never reached the consignee. On August 18th, Supt. Bown and Sergt. Buckley searched the prisoner Pages's house, and found a number of neckties and a leather bag concealed under a bed in one of the bed rooms. Subsequently they searched Florence's house, and the Superintendent found two bags underneath one bed, and a bundle of ties underneath another. On the following day Supt. Bowen and Police-constable Spendlove searched Bull's house, and Spendlove found a couple of ties. The ties and bags found were now identified by Messrs. Coates, S. Herratt jun., and J. Herratt. The prisoners were committed for trial on the charge, and reserved their defence.

William Loverock, of Horninglow, and John Florence, one of the prisoners in the previous case, were then charged with stealing a case containing forty-three boxes of cigars, value £16, on July 27th, the property of the London and North-Western Railway Company. Mr Hockin of Euston, prosecuted; Mr Hextell, of Derby, appeared for Loverock, and Mr. Wilson defended Florence. A man named Harvey had also been arrested, but no evidence was offered against him and he was therefore discharged. On July 24th a case of cigars was consigned by Messrs. Thorns, Son, and Co, cigar importers, of Boston, Lincolnshire, to Mr Smith, of Birmingham, but the case never reached its destination. Mr Hockin stated that he should be able to show that it left Derby all right, but was missing at Burton. After proving the delivery of the case to the company, he called Rowland Henry Hale, landlord of the Crescent Hotel, Horninglow-street, who deposed that on the 5th instant he met Loverock driving along the Derby-road in a gig. After they had passed each other Loverock pulled up and asked him if he wanted to purchase any cigars. He replied "It all depends: are they all right?" Loverock said "Yes, they are all right, and the price is 6s per box". He (witness) said he could do with some, but he should like to see them first, as there was so much deception in cigars. Loverock promised to let him see some, and they then parted. In the evening of the same day the prisoners went to his house – in a conveyance, he believed – and showed him eighteen boxes of cigars wrapped up in canvas. They all three went in the smoke-room and he (witness) tested three samples of the cigars and then offered to purchase a few of the boxes. Loverock told him he had better have the lot; they would do him good, and if he would take them all he would reduce the price by a shilling a box. He (witness) therefore purchased the eighteen boxes, and gave the money – £4 10s – to Florence. Cross-examined: There were only three sorts of cigars among the eighteen boxes. Loverock told him they were a bankrupt's stock from Derby

and that he had £40 worth. He gave the cigars up to Police-constable
Freeman on Thursday. Florence took the money, and Loverock did not
say anything against him having it. He thought that as he had made
all the arrangements with Loverock, he (Loverock) should have the
money. He had known Loverock for two years and knew that his father
was a large farmer at Horninglow. He had never had any business
transactions with Loverock before. He should not have purchased
the cigars except on Loverock's recommendation. He believed that
Loverock had told him as to where he had the cigars from – Four of
the boxes produced were identified by private marks as a portion of
the case, and the other boxes were sworn to as containing the same
quality of cigars as those which were alleged to have been stolen. –
Mr Hockin said he could not complete the case that day, and he must,
therefore, apply for an adjournment for a week. – Mr Hextall said he
could not oppose the application, but he must ask the magistrates to
grant bail. His client held a most respectable position and could offer
substantial bail. At present, too, the case was only one of suspicion. –
Mr Hockin replied that he was instructed to oppose bail. Only a little
over thirty out of the forty-three boxes had been found, and if the
prisoner was liberated he might interfere to prevent the finding of the
other boxes – Mr Hextall imagined that it would be to the advantage
of his client to assist the police as far as he could, and he was quite
willing to do so, but he had no knowledge as to the whereabouts of
the other missing goods. He could not deny that his client had been
dealing with the cigars, but it might be shown that he was doing so in
a legitimate manner and without any knowledge of how the cigars had
been procured. With only a prima facie case of possession against his
client, he thought that bail ought to be granted. – Sir Tonman Mosley
remarked that he should have been glad to have granted bail if he had
thought it ought to be granted. Under the circumstances he did not see
how he could allow the prisoner to be liberated; at all events, not until
the whole of the evidence had been heard – The two prisoners were
then remanded for a week. We understand that some more tobacco has
been found on Florence's premises.

Burton News and Standard – Thursday December 5, 1889

Burglary in Station Street

Another Remand

John Florence, hawker, Horninglow Street, and Charles Rawson, out-porter, New Street, were again charged with breaking into and entering the shop of Mr. Marks, tobacconist, Station Street, and stealing therefrom 116lbs of tobacco and £20 in money.

Mr. Marks having repeated his evidence which has already been reported.

Henry Florence, labourer and son to the prisoner, John Florence, said he lived with his father in Marriott's yard, Horninglow Street. On the morning of Nov, 8th, someone came and knocked at the door, shouting out "Jack, come down." His father opened the window and asked who was there, and, what he was wanted for. The voice below said "Come down, we have got a bit of a job for you." His father replied that as it was not the time he would not go down, and then the witness afterwards opened the window himself and saw Rawson standing about three yards from it. He (Rawson) importuned the elder Florence to come down, and he complied after some persuasion. Witness then heard Rawson say to some other person "It is all right, Tucker, wheel it down the garden," and at the same time observed them wheeling something on a hand-barrow in the direction indicated.

Sergt. Price deposed that in company with P.e. Buggy, he was at the railway station on the 21st ult from about 6.30 till 8 o'clock… Same as last report.

A man named Wagstaff, residing in Horninglow Street, had been arrested by Police-constable Bourke on suspicion of being concerned in a railway robbery, but as no evidence was offered against him he was discharged. – Mr Briggs, of Derby, had been instructed to appear for Wagstaff, and he asked upon what grounds his client had been arrested – Mr Supt. Brown remarked that Wagstaff was the father of one of the prisoners who was committed last week, and, he being suspected, his house was searched, and a quantity of silk and cloth and a number of handkerchiefs &c were found. He was unable to give any satisfactory account of his possession, and was therefore, arrested – He also contended that the police-officer had no right to search the house without a warrant, and he should report the matter to the Chief Constable. His client had been a respectable position under Messrs. Allsopp and Sons for twenty years, and it was not right that he should have been locked up in the illegal way in which he had been. Mr Supt Bowen stated that patterns of the cloth had been taken and the Midland Railway Company's detectives were endeavouring to trace from where it had come. If they were successful Wagstaff would in all probability be again arrested.

The court was crowded during the hearing of the case.

Burton Weekley News and General Advertiser – Thursday, September 5, 1878

"The Railway Robberies"

William Loverock and John Florence were brought up on remand, charged with having stolen 43 boxes of cigars, value £16 – Mr. Hockin of Euston, prosecuted, and Mr Hextall defended Loverock, and Mr Wilson defended Florence. In addition to the evidence taken last week –

William West, carter, proved receiving the case of cigars from Messrs Thorn, Son and Co, of Boston, and he delivered it to the Great Northern Railway Station.

Joseph Pilkington, checker, in the employ of the Railway Company at Boston, proved receiving the goods from West, and he weighed the case of cigars. Its weight was 3 qrs 15lbs. On the day following its receipt (24th of June), he saw it loaded into wagon 2394, labelled to Derby.

Albert Pratt, late a check at Derby Station, said on the 26th of July, he transferred some goods from wagon 2394 to wagon 3472, belonging to the North Staffordshire Railway Company, labelled to Burton. Amongst the goods there was a case of cigars for Smith, of Birmingham. It was in good condition.

John Adams, a loader in the employ of the London North Eastern Railway Company, at Burton, said on the 27th of July be unloaded some goods from wagon 3472, and loaded them into another wagon. He found on his "loading slip" a case of cigars for Smith, of Birmingham, and on examining it, he found it to be empty, and he made a remark to that effect.

David Price, a clerk in the employ of the London and North Western Railway Company, at Burton, said he received the "loading Slip" from the last witness, and from the remark on it he put on the invoice, opposite the case for Smith, "Empty when received at Burton".

William Henry Smith said he was an estate agent residing at Birmingham. He ordered 43 boxes of cigars from Messrs Thorn, Son and Co, of Boston in June last. He never received the cigars. The empty case was sent. The value of the cigars was £16 14s 6d.

Joseph Potter, landlord of the Forester's Arms, Horninglow, said about a month ago the defendant Loverock came to his house at night, and said 'Do you want some cigars'. He replied 'I am not badly in want of them, but I think I can do with a box or two', and the defendant then fetched some cigars out of a trap which was standing at the door, and he bought eight boxes from him, for which he paid from £2 4s. He afterwards delivered them to P.e. Freeman. He saw him again the following day, and he asked him whether the cigars were all right, and he said they were as they were park of bankruptcy stock – Cross-examined: He had known Loverock for some years. From the time he sold the cigars up to the time he was apprehended, he was constantly in the neighbourhood.

P.e. Freeman said on the 22nd ult, he received 13 boxes of cigars from Mr Hales, and afterwards eight more on the same day from the last witness. He arrested Loverock at 11.30 the same night. On charging him with stealing the cigars, he replied "I don't knew anything about them" – Cross Examined: Loverock was going towards home when he was arrested. When arrested he charged him with stealing the cigars, and not with having received them, knowing them to be stolen.

Barry Parsons, detective, in the employ of London and North Western Railway, said he charged the defendant Florence with the theft, and he pleaded not guilty.

Mr Hextall said there was no evidence that the defendants had stolen the cigars, and asked the Bench if they thought there was sufficient to justify them in sending the defendants for trial at the next Starrd Quarter Sessions, about the middle of October.

Mr Hextell then applied of bail on the behalf of Loverock, and the bench, after considering the application, granted it, two sureties being accepted in £100 each, and himself in £200.

"Local and District News"
The Railway Robberies – In these cases, tried on Tuesday, Wagstaff and Page were sentenced to nine months imprisonment each; Florence to ten months; Ball to twelve months; and Loverock to seven months imprisonment.

Burton News – Thursday July 15, 1880
Larcery of a Spade – Joseph Page (44), labourer, of Clay Mills, and John Florence, labourer, or Horninglow-street, were charged with having about a month ago stolen a spade, value 2s, the property of the Burton Town Council – Mr Mears defended – From the evidence it appeared the constables (P.e.s Buggy and Snape) went to search the home of the defendant Joseph Page on suspicion of having stolen it he said the spade was taken to his home by Florence and this Florence admitted, and at the same time he strongly asserted that the spade was his private property. On arresting Florence he made several attempts to escape, and also bit the finger of P.e. Snape, and behaved in a violent manner. – For the defence it was contended that the spade had been in the possess of Florence for a considerable period, over a year, and after witnesses had been heard, they were committed to take their trial at the Stafford Assizes.

Burton News and Standard – Thursday, April 4, 1889
Making People Fly – John Florence, hawker, Horninglow Street, was summoned by P.C. Harthill, on a charge of furiously driving a horse and wagon through the Market Place, on the 23rd ult. – The constable stated

that the defendant "made people fly in all directions". Witness spoke to him about his conduct, but without avail. – Sergt. Austin corroborated – The bench fined him 10s and 102 6d costs, or 14 days imprisonment with hard labour.

Burton News and Standard – Thursday, November 28, 1889
The Recent Burglary at a Tobacconist's Shop
Capture of Some of the Booty and The Supposed Thieves
At the borough police court on Friday, before Councillor Turner at P.B. Mason, Esq. John Florence, hawker, Horninglow Street, and Charles Rawson, out-porter, New Street, were charged with breaking into and entering the shop of Mr Marks, tobacconist, Station Street, and stealing therefrom 116lbs of tobacco and £20 in money. The prosecuter stated that on the night of the 8th inst, his shop was locked up by his son. There were at the time in the cellar behind the shop 150lbs of tobacco in boxes, while about £20 in silver and copper were in his desk drawer. Next morning when he got to the shop, which was a lock-up place, he found the back door had been wrenched open, two locks having been forced. The desk drawer had been removed and emptied, and placed on a chair. All the cash had been extracted, nothing but a cheque being left. He examined the tobacco produced (consisting of 112lbs of thick and thin twist and he had no doubt that it was part of the tobacco stolen from his shop – P.C. Price deposed that in company with P.C. Buggy he was at the railway station last Thursday night from about 6.30 till eight o'clock. About five minutes to eight he saw the prisoner Florence and a gentleman get out of a cab at the station, and the basket produced was on the top of the cab. There was some pots and straw at the top of the basket to make it appear like a basket of earthenware. It was taken on the platform by a porter, and Florence and the gentleman he had mentioned also went on the platform. When the train came in the basket was about to be put in the guard's van when witness went up and said to Florence "What there is there I have bought off Florence". Witness said he believed it was tobacco that had been stolen, and he should take possession of it. The man with Florence said he had bought the

tobacco off Florence as smuggled tobacco. He then took Florence into custody and brought him to the police-station, where he charged him with breaking into and entering Mr Mark's shop and stealing therefrom the missing money and tobacco. He replied "I didn't break into the shop, but I think I may as well tell you who did. About half past five in the morning about a fortnight ago a man they call Charley and another man came to my house and knocked me up. Charley said "Come down Jack, I want to speak to you". When I came down I saw they had got a quantity of tobacco on a barrow. I said 'Oh…, where have you had that from'. Charley said "Oh, never you mind, you shove it out of the road somewhere". When he then took it down the garden and buried it". Witness went on to say that he arrested Rawson ("Charley"), and brought him to the police-station, and Florence said he was the man who had brought him the tobacco, but Rawson denied the accusation. Witness then charged the prisoners jointly with the offence already named. – At the request of Supt. Gilbride both.

HOLY LAND TRIP: 21ST–28TH NOVEMBER 2011

My wife Anne, made a trip in 2009 to Epworth, the spiritual home of John Wesley (Methodist) in celebration of Charles Wesley (his brother), who many of you will recall writing so many hundreds of well-known hymns. On her way back, Revd Phil Gough gave her a leaflet about a trip to the Holy Land, led by Rob Cotton, Martin Turner, Tony Miles, Ann Hall, Phil Gough, Pam Rhodes and Dave Bilbrough, to be called Biblefresh. Her first words, when she got home, were to say, "If only we could go." Anyone that knows me well would have thought, "No, he'll not bother," but straightaway I was keen. I rang Christian Tours, paid a deposit, and set about getting a passport, and before long we both were at Luton Airport and on our way to what was to be a dream holiday.

The first day was spent on a boat in the calm of the Sea of Galilee. We went out to the middle of the sea accompanied by another boat belonging to our group, which was then tied together with prayers, readings and many hymns being sung. Mostly Methodists, we could certainly make a great noise. My, what a service! And with Pam Rhodes leading everyone, it was fantastic! I spoke with Pam whilst still on the boat (see photograph) and she confirmed her patronage of the Much Hoole Woodland Burial Ground. I just felt that God was with us!

We at first stayed at Bethsaida and halfway through moved onto Bethlehem, and, of course, we were then behind the dividing wall (boundary). None of us ever felt in the least danger. I will sometime, in another book, go over details more thoroughly as I am under much pressure to send the manuscript off; and I hope, in 2015/2016, to take a group there myself, and if anyone is interested then please get in touch.

I will just mention a few other experiences that we were involved in. After the sail on Galilee, we travelled to where the River Jordan begins. Some people were submerged in the River Jordan. We visited Caesarea Philippi where we understand that they may have found the foundations of the first church where Jesus said to Peter, "I want you to build my church here." This is near to Galilee, about 100 yards away, so I went routing under the water's edge where Jesus may have walked into the water to cool his feet, and brought home three pieces of stone from that spot.

It was very moving when one of our ministers gave the Sermon on the Mount (the Mount of Beatitudes).

We also visited Masada, which was a most moving experience, and you must see the film with Peter O'Toole and Anthony Quayle playing the leading parts, or indeed try to visit it sometime. I shall surely go back again.

We stopped at the Dead Sea, and some went in the water.

We carried the Cross on its mile long route through the Old City of Jerusalem and visited the Mayor and the Mayor's Reception for us, and visited the Wailing Wall.

We visited Nof Ginosar to see the 2000-year-old boat named the 'Jesus Boat' which was unearthed from the Sea of Galilee. Of course, at the time, Jesus was around.

We went to the Church of the Nativity and drove past the Shepherds Fields, with all the wonderful thoughts of Christmas that they reminded us of. We did so many things.

One of the most moving parts was to go down steps into a dungeon where we were told Jesus spent his last night—the metalwork is still there—and we saw the site of the Garden Tomb.

I must also add that a wedding took place just yards away from where we queued to see where Jesus was born—unbelievable!

Finally, I had it in my mind that as I was building a church, I must try and get two pieces of wood to make a cross. I spoke with Mike the guide, who said "no trouble", and that I must go with him to a joiner's workshop to see what I was buying. What an awful dusty place. It cost me £100, but you can now see the cross at Much Hoole. Great!

We never saw, or heard of, any trouble, but according to a Christian shopkeeper near one of our hotels, it would appear (if you believe the man) that the Palestinian people are the ones being persecuted, and that some of them are going to Brazil. I don't think for football either! And, like I said, I will again write more when I have been a second time.

SIR TOM FINNEY CBE (1922–2014)— PRESTON NORTH END

It is a great privilege that Tom's son, Brian, has given me permission to place his father's photograph on the front cover of my book, and I now want to say a few heartfelt words about Tom the footballer, and the Tom that I knew through my business. It is, as you would imagine, a story of much praise.

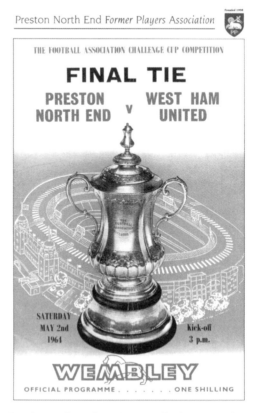

Catalogue from the 1964 cup final – I was there

I have resisted writing snippets from the many books I have read that I could have used, and part way through I shall write a little of Preston North End's fall from grace as that was the era that I sat through as a season ticket holder.

It would be when I was nine that we all played under the street lights in Out Lane, Croston, and on the field next door to Mum's (owned by the local publican of the Lord Nelson pub and farmer Reggie Cottam, who only used it for grazing his old horse Duke, who must have been twenty-six years old then; and when we heard the horse feet coming, led by Reggie, off we ran like mice so he would not see us).

At about twelve years old, my brother's boss would take us both to watch Preston and, of course, Tom Finney. By that time, Preston had lost the Cup Final. I did not see that, but by all accounts Tommy Docherty and Tom had a poor match. It seems that Tom never got the ball where he wanted it, but they were up against Derek Kevan, Ronnie Allan, Ray Barlow—and *they* were no mugs!

Three years later, I started work, and two good lads worked with me at Richard Hunt's Joiners: Abel Watkinson and Sydney Wright, who travelled to matches at Deepdale on Fishwick buses, and I tagged along. We always stood behind the Town End goal where we met up with Jonathan Jackson and the Chadwick family. In those days, the *Lancashire Evening Post* had its own football editions which would be in the newsagents shops by 6.00 p.m. Now, that is long since gone, and just one daily evening paper is printed the night before these days. The football edition newspaper then retained a marvellous reporter called Walter Pilkington whose Friday night late news had us all fanatics, looking to see if PNE had bought a new player, or was Tom in or was Tom out, and if Tom was injured there would be no such news given out as that would reduce the crowd by about 5000 people.

My memory is still quite good, but if I have got the wrong dates then please bear with me. Now here are a few matches that stick in my mind near the finish of Tom's career.

Does anybody recall the game against Birmingham City where Preston scored nine goals and they all went past the current England goalkeeper Gil Merrick? Match after match, it was four, five, six goals, most of them put on a plate—yes, you've guessed, by Tom! The great Nottingham Forest side who reached the Cup Final—I think against Luton Town—what a defence they had, with Jack McKinley at centre half and Jack Bond and Jack Burkitt as full backs, all well over six feet tall. Every ball from the goalkeeper was sent to them first and they then passed it upfield. They played one of the best matches I ever saw.

Preston North End played Blackpool, Burnley, Bolton—very keenly fought local derbys. My word, that Bolton team possessed some strong lads—Hartley, Higgins, Banks, and Tom's longtime friend Nat Lofthouse; but he would join with his Bolton mates and would show no mercy to Tom.

Plus that leather ball!

Does anybody recall the match in 1959, when we went to Chelsea to play their great team of youth players, where we drew 4–4, and they came back to Deepdale and beat us 4–5? Where, and this is hard to believe, Jimmy Greaves scored all nine of Chelsea's goals. When you think of Webb, Osgood, Jimmy Greaves, Bonetti, Tambling, Harris, Hollins, it was a great team which maybe would have beaten the Chelsea of today, and yet our youth team got to the final against them. We had George Ross, Peter Thompson, Dave Wilson, Alan Spavin, Gordon Milne, with John Barton in goal, who was one of the youngest players ever to play in Division One in those days. At that time, Tommy Thompson and Sammy Taylor were in fine form. I think Tommy was top scorer in Division One, one year, or thereabouts. Tom Finney was to become, twice, footballer of the year—a fantastic feat. All in all, Preston were top entertainers in football but it had to come to an end, and against Sid Owen's Luton Town, on the 30th April 1960 (with me, Geoffrey, sat on cinders behind the Town End goal), and 30,000 people crammed in, Tom said his farewells and grown men and women wept.

In 1961, Fred Else (a really good goalkeeper) was transferred to Blackburn Rovers, and with my now having my own transport, I then went to Ewood, home of Blackburn Rovers, to see some night matches.

I saw Rovers thrash the great Tottenham Hotspur side who did the double. What a great match, and I got quite fond of seeing Ronnie Clayton, and Matt Woods, play—he was a dream centre half. I am told Fred Else was never as good at Blackburn, following an injury.

I also used to watch Southport and remember Bryan Griffiths—he was too good to play in the Fourth Division.

To come back to Preston, they were relegated in 1961 with Jimmy Milne taking charge. We did have about five years of excitement, nearly bouncing straight back into the First Division; having big battles against Leeds with 30,000 inside Deepdale, and I mean battles! My goodness, they were a rough team.

We finished third with being just short of two class players, but we did have the pleasure of Alex Dawson, Nobby Lawton, Howard Kendal, George Ross, and Tony Singleton; especially Tony with that remarkable goal from inside his own half at Villa Park in the semi-final of the Cup against Swansea, when he kicked the ball over the goalkeeper from sixty-odd yards to reach the Cup Final with West Ham United. The Final was a fantastic day out. We put up a good fight, had a couple of early chances, and if they had gone in, who knows what would have happened; but when you look at the West Ham side, half of them played for England, so then you cannot be so sad.

Alex Dawson's penalties were worth the admission price alone. We were to draw big teams out of what was the First Division for the FA Cup, and had many tussles with Man United and Liverpool. No wonder Liverpool bought Peter Thompson and Gordon Milne and, at a later date, Mark Lawrenson and Howard Kendall went to Everton. After that, we went down and down and down till we had to reapply to get back into the Fourth Division—my God, where did it all go wrong? I often wonder, where did all the money go when we were once averaging 30,000 crowds?

Tom Finney later made an appearance on *This Is Your Life* with film star Peter O'Toole, both of whom were in the Second World War together.

Bobby Charlton and David Beckham did play for us at Deepdale.

And things looked up when David Moyes and Bryan Gray took charge, and we got to quite a few play-offs but didn't make it. In all, we have failed nine times to get promotion, including once again this year (2014).

MY PERSONAL DEALINGS WITH TOM FINNEY

My first close-up with Tom was working as an apprentice joiner in Birchwood Avenue, Hutton, near Preston in 1959, with Tom fixing the cast-iron gutters and downspouts. In those days it was done with red lead and putty to seal the joints—no mention then of Health and Safety!

Years later I was in hospital—the old Royal Infirmary—and Tom walked through with someone who appeared to be a Clerk of Works, to look at replacing some old toilets. I can still picture that day—Tom still playing, and all those really sick men; without doubt they would have leapt out of bed and kissed his feet if they could have. They would remember that moment until they died. I ask, would David Beckham and Georgie Best have done that, with no security on hand? It was so unreal then and still would be now.

Many times I was to see him representing the club and attending relatives' funerals. He was to become a magistrate and health executive at the new hospital now being called Royal Preston Hospital.

My hearse driver was Frank Gornall, who played for Preston reserves and, but for the war, would have played for the first team, but did once play for Portsmouth first team. Frank was a keen supporter of the Ex-Players Association who used to get together now and again, and once I went with him, and his son Mark, to reminisce about the Cup Final against West Ham United which was held at a local hotel called "The Pines", Chorley, where about eight ex-West Ham former footballers came all the way 'up north' to meet Tom in person. They all called him 'Boss', and about nine who played for Preston in the final also came to the do. It was a truly inspiring evening, blessed with the appearance of Sir Tom.

Rt. Rev Bishop John Goddard, followed by Tom Hoyle, John Hall and Rev. Stephen Poxon (National President)

Digging of the turf

A few years ago I was very fortunate to get his agreement to do some promotional work for me whilst getting the Much Hoole Woodland Burial Ground consecrated. He gave me his private phone number, and we arranged a time to go to his home and bring him back to do an interview. The fact that he walked on the grounds also made it, in my eyes, hallowed ground—what a thrill. He said it was "a lovely place" (see photograph).

Tom Finney pictured at Much Hoole Woodland Burial Ground

My, he never stopped talking about what it was like to play for England, having to get his own tickets and having to meet up in (say) Liverpool railway station with other lads, and then to travel to wherever, and coming home with every bone in his body aching and having to be up for work the next day. He did say it was more frightening finding his way on the train as a young fella to Liverpool than facing these big rough fullbacks! All inspiring stuff!

He also gave me his thoughts on his friends Nat Lofthouse, Bobby Charlton, Roger Taylor, Duncan Edwards, Tommy Docherty, Stanley

Matthews, Bill Shankley, and Ronnie Clayton. He told me Duncan Edwards was something special, and how he used to chuckle to himself when he heard Bill Shankley say to people "Tom could pass them with one leg or with his overcoat on". Matt Busby was also a huge admirer of him.

He spoke about his dear wife Elsie a lot as well. He then started to reminisce about local characters where I live, in that he knew the Orritt family in Walmer Bridge. At that time, Walmer Bridge had a great team of football amateurs and I think they filled three quarters of their team. He thought that some could have made it into the league. He also said he was forever doing presentational awards, being booked by Tommy Orritt, who was a local business man. He said that so many requests were being made by Tommy, he could have done with an agent.

I must also add that Sir Tom's birthday is the same date as that of my daughter Andrea (5th April), who you will have read about earlier in this book.

A local friend, Ken Rigby, who is an expert on Preston North End, has given me help and I am most grateful.

You would never would have thought that when I was playing in the street and under the lights, I should have become so involved and so honoured.

Sir Tom—well done, thou good and faithful man.

As I near the end of my book I must mention by name some good people, friends and ministers who have been a great help in many ways:

Norman Ditchfield, who was a great help when I first became an undertaker, as was also his daughter, Elsie.

The Dandy family, especially John and Bill.

Norman and Nellie Caunce—a friendship that Anne and I have cherished a long time.

I remember good neighbours of Mum's: the Iddon family, both Forrest families, Florence and Roy Dickinson, and Jack Dickinson and family. I have already mentioned Sally, Francis and Elizabeth Jackson, Nellie and Jim Norris. How they made mother feel important.

My grandsons Christopher and Jonathan at a signing session with Tom Finney

Sir Tom Finney in my home

Croston was truly a unique place. Having already mentioned Billy Meadows, I must add Carole Trafford, Winn Singleton, Jean Hampson, John and Josie Rayner, the Kearton family, the Barlow family, Jack Hutton, Annie and Jean Hesketh, Ned and Annie Jackson, Dick and Nanny Cottam, Margaret Knight, the Whittle family, and the Norcross family, Norman and Dorothy Edmondson, the Eatock family, Judith Gray and Ian.

I must also mention Tom and Ada Dalton, one of my first and best customers in joinery work. The love they had together was unbelievable. Ada doted on Tom and that was returned when Ada became ill. I witnessed that when I took Tom to visit Ada in hospital. He was a good horseman, and it was a privilege to take one of my stallions to his funeral.

Min Coxhead and her lovely family—they couldn't pay me soon enough for any work I did for them. I still meet Kathleen and her daughter—what good people they were and are.

Also, the Smith family who took over our farm. Colin and Maurice Ellison and their father Clarence, Pat and Bill Martland, and Alan Roby. Good people!

And not forgetting others too numerous to mention.

Plus, further afield, dear Mary Atkinson, Cliff and Cath Greenlees, and Edward Jackson.

To all our friends at Much Hoole Chapel, a most special thank you to Jim Brown and Olive Cork for their support over the years.

Thanks to Mr and Mrs Gaskell for looking after all the paperwork, and to Steve Davies for helping with the horses. Without his weekly visits, plus his driving, I probably would never have been where I am today.

I must also mention the friendship with Pam Rhodes, her husband Richard, and Lily, my agent. We are so grateful.

I must thank Richard Bramley (architect) for all his patience and the stress that I have caused him.

One can always say good things about relatives, but I must mention cousin Kathleen for always being at the end of a phone for a natter, and her recent sad loss of Norman.

Frances and James Stout have also been very much involved in everything that we have done, be it work or charities. Without embarrassing Frances, I am very close to her. It's something that has just grown and grown. It was sad to lose James some time ago, but she copes fairly well. Of course, she is of the old Sylvia Whalley strain, and I think dearly of her and her family.

Having worked with ministers all my life, I must mention Revd Francis Bruce (yes, of the famous Scottish name). I was his number one undertaker for a long time and used to marvel at how he took charge, either in the home of a deceased, or in church at the funeral service. Together with his dear wife, Fiona, they have remained good friends of our family.

Revd David Day was equally a major influence on our family and others. He was a great visitor and did a wonderful funeral service and, of course, weddings and christenings. He died in Yorkshire, but it was a great honour to carry him at his funeral. That man! Whilst a P.O.W. in Burma, though he was not a minister then, he used to secretly give Communion out of a tin can. What faith amongst all that cruelty! He was a butcher before coming into the Church, and people will find it hard to believe that very early in a morning (just before Christmas) he came and helped me pluck turkeys. Together with his lovely wife, Doris, they were good friends to many and gave us great support with Andrea.

Paster Ronald Witts and his dear wife Ann; for many years they looked after the people of Bretherton. Ron and Ann lost their son, David, in a car accident near Skipton and I was privileged to conduct the funeral. Anne and I did become close friends. I was later to conduct Ron's funeral, and we wish Ann all our best. It hasn't been easy for her, but I know she has a good close family.

I have also been privileged to work with other good ministers such as Martyn Rogers, Andrew Parkinson, Peter Taylor, Ted Pullan, David Reynolds, Tom Thompson, and Revd K Bounds who married Anne and I—a Godly man.

Finally, two ministers who some years ago made an instant and lasting impression on us the Whalley family: firstly, Revd Harry Pugh who I would rate very highly. Harry had a presence about him where he appeared to be on everybody's level, and did much good, in my opinion, for our village. He was also a great supporter of the Much Hoole Country Fair. It was sad that he didn't stay too long, but we still think highly of him. Revd Yvonne Pearson came into our lives at the time of Alisa's illness and she became a rock to us and to many others. I think Much Hoole Chapel would have closed but for her. I recall Paster Ronald Witts' request for her to take his funeral service, which she did.

You will recall the name of George Iddon earlier in this book. When George died, his daughter Christine asked if we could get someone to play a brass instrument. We were struggling to find someone, and then thought of Yvonne, who agreed to play the trumpet. She also played at the Daniel O'Donnell concert. Good on you, Yvonne!

Having written the above out for Janice to type, I have decided that I must mention other friends that I have picked up along the way: Eric Trafford, Mrs Green, Mr Higginson, Derek McClusky, Bob and Bessie Tuson, Colin and Jean Seed, Mrs Addis, Mr Greenwood, John and Jenny Barron, the Rigby family, the Baker family, the Stopforth family, Jean Norris, June Faulkner and Jan, Mr and Mrs Pooley, Morag Roberts and Fiona, Jim and Mary Taylor (née Wrennall, friends of my wife's mother).

I went to Secondary School and knew Mary West, and have carried out the funerals of her father and brother. As we go to print, Mary (now Mary Davies) has sadly died and she is now buried in the Woodland Burial Ground, not fifty yards from my door. She leaves a loving husband and was a dear mother to two daughters.

And finally, to the Miller family of Tarleton, who have just lost dad and mum Ruth—all of them from good farming stock. They also have two of the best DIY shops—one in Parbold and another in Tarleton—and they are to stock this book for which I am eternally grateful.

In every business you get awkward customers and I was no different. There must be about ten people/families who tried to do me down, and most of it led to my suffering financial hardship, but they know who they are. Enough said.

On Thursday 3rd September, 1.00 p.m., I confirmed onsite with Peter Baldwin, of Heskin Fabrications, Leyland (a small firm that I know well), an order for seven Portland steel frames which were to be delivered in three weeks time for the new chapel. The dream rolled on and on and I hoped that we could get the top on for winter, or at least the roof, felt and battens before January 2010.

I hope this book is not too sad. Having just read a book about all the suffering that the Jewish people went through in the last war, even those in hiding, makes some of my struggle seem to be of no significance.

For those younger folk setting off in life, remember this: learn your English and Maths, be well-mannered to your own and peer groups, and keep yourself tidy (soap and water still isn't very expensive), watch the drink and fatty foods and, finally, try and play team games. You could be pleasantly surprised when you attend an interview for work—you may get the job!

I have, at the time of reading this proof, buried nearly 400 people in the woodland burial ground, and can I ask if you would remember three young people who lie nearby—Donna, Oliver and Joseph—whose parents miss them immensely.

In September 2013, the dream continued in that I received planning permission to extend God's Acre Chapel by two thirds, on green belt land, to form an Ecumenical Educational School/Centre, complete with auxiliary rooms, in which our chaplain, Revd Malcolm Maymand, will take charge, with a team of helpers which is made up of Mrs Kathleen Cooper, a very much respected layperson in the Catholic faith in Preston; Preston's leading business lady, Ms Margaret Mason, florist and national events organiser in flowers; Ms Mary Layfield who has spent a lifetime in nursing and pastoral working; and to complete the team, me and my wife Anne as backup. It is being overseen by the Rt Revd John Goddard, Bishop of Burnley, for which we are indeed blessed. It is hoped we can have at least eight students, who will take part in ten courses with the best being helped to carry on into the ministry. Our patron, Pam Rhodes, laid the foundation stone on 29th March 2014.

Pam Rhodes leading the dedication

The Chaplain Rev. Malcolm Maymand

Pam Rhodes with husband, Richard leading the singing

The laying of the foundation stone for the Educational Centre

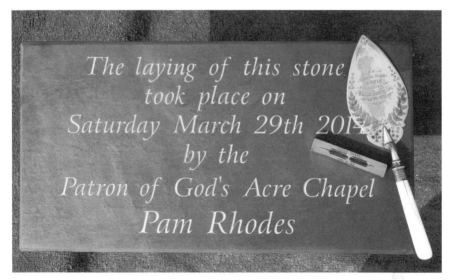

Foundation stone laid by Pam Rhodes on 29th March, 2014

Pam Rhodes in the Preston Guild Fishers of Men float accompanied by friends of Much Hoole Methodist Church

Pam Rhodes, patron of God's Acre Chapel

I hope those of you that remember Marjory Whalley will just think for a moment about her and how she had to work so hard all her life. I also hope that you have found this book interesting.

Yours in dreaming

Geoff Whalley.